FRONT COVER: Chesham a century ago, from Dungrove.

Buck   **The Towne and parrish of great Chessam**

A booke of Taxaton or rate made the tenth day of June 1606 in the fourth yere of the Raigne of o[ur] Soveraigne Lord King James by those whose names are before specified Assembled together that daye according to the makinge and knowledge before geven openlye in the Church vppon the Saboth dayes the first of June and agaunst the sight of the same for the rate[?] of all the inhabitants of the said Towne and pishe of great Chessam for contribution and payment of money towards the repayring of the Church and for other occasions concerning the same.

The Rate weekly to the Poore   *The single rate*

ob.q	S[i]r Edmund Ashfelde knight	iij s. vj d.
q ob q	Thomas Ashfold esquier	iiij s. vj d.
ob q	Richard Bowle gent	iij s. vj d.
ob q	William Woodon of Hundridge gent	iij s. vj d. iij d.
q	Mathew Chase of Hundridge gent	iij s. vj d.
ob q	Richard Ward of whelpleyhill	iij d.
q	John Turner of Ashley grene	iij s. vj d. iij d.
q	John Grover of whelpleyhill	ij s. vj d.
q	Richard Cakefold of Ashridge	ij s. vj d.
q	M[r] Thomas Ashfold of Ashridge gent	ij s. vj d.
q	Stephen Grover of the same	ij s. vij d.

'A booke of Taxaton or rate made the fourth day of June 1606 . . .'

A CHESHAM CENTURY

The story of a Town and its Council 1894-1994

by
Arnold H. J. Baines MA PhD FSA FRHistS
and Clive Birch FSA FRSA
assisted by George Malin, Mike Kennedy
and Steve James,
with additional pictures by John Armistead

BARON
MCMXCIV

PUBLISHED BY BARON BIRCH FOR QUOTES LIMITED
AND PRODUCED BY KEY COMPOSITION,
SOUTH MIDLANDS LITHOPLATES, CHENEY & SONS,
RAVEN PRINT & WBC BOOKBINDERS

© Arnold H. J. Baines & C. F. W. Birch 1994

All rights reserved. No part of this publication may be reproduced, stored in a retrieval system, or transmitted, in any form or by any means, electronic, mechanical, photocopying, recording or otherwise, without the prior permission of Quotes Limited.

Any copy of this book issued by the Publisher as clothbound or as a paperback is sold subject to the condition that it shall not by way of trade or otherwise, be lent, re-sold, hired out or otherwise circulated without the Publisher's prior consent, in any form of binding or cover other than that in which it is published, and without a similar condition including this condition being imposed on a subsequent purchaser.

ISBN 0 86023 549 1

KEY TO CAPTION CREDITS

The majority of old pictures come from the Editor's collection or John Armistead's files. Modern pictures were taken by John. Portraits of Chairmen are produced from the Town Council archives. Some of the older pictures were originally lent for copying, and we are grateful to Mrs Bristow (MB), Enea Batchelor (EB), Mrs L. Moulder (LM), Peter Larkin (PL and HS/PL — from an original by Hector Smith), Mr Warner (W), London Transport (LTE) and James Venn for past access to the Stanley H. Freese Collection (SHF).

Contents

Acknowledgements	6
Foreword	7
Introduction	8

Arnold Baines:
One Thousand Years 10
Eighteen Ninety Four 31
A Chesham Century
1894-1974 35

Michael Kennedy:
1974-1994 89

George Malin:
Wise Counsels 94

Steve James:
Serve One Another 98

Clive Birch:
A Town for Today 107

Appendix: Chairmen and Clerks 138

Index 139
Subscribers 143

ACKNOWLEDGEMENTS

This book was conceived by councillors, backed by the Council, encouraged by two Mayors, researched by the Clerk, a past Mayor, the principal author and the editor, written by a past Chairman of the UDC and former Town Mayor, past Treasurer and Clerk, present Mayor and a past editor of the *Examiner*. It includes the memories of Chesham historians, writers, councillors, a policeman, founder-Tabler, farmer, landlady, Countess, a Star Yarder, head teacher, Bury daughter, Bishop, engineer and two local editors.

Specifically, the main text was researched and written by Chesham's leading authority on the town's past, Arnold Baines, who was also twice Chairman of the UDC, Mayor, and still serves as a Councillor, a position he has held for 41 years. We are all in his debt. Past Treasurer and Clerk George Malin and present Mayor Steve James each contributed a chapter. Town Clerk Mike Kennedy has held all the threads together from the beginning, and without his tact and tenacity the book would not have happened. He was aided and abetted by past councillor and Mayor, Bernard Meldrum, who spent many hours delving into volumes of minutes and providing admirable summaries of significant facts.

Chesham folk, past and present, have helped in many ways, and most are recorded with their own words, in the final chapter. We are grateful for their contributions, especially Peter Larkin, founder-Tabler, who also lent several pictures and offered wise counsel. My first landlady, Rosie Wood, now Alison Horsnell, spurred me on, and my old friend John Armistead looked out extra pictures and took more specially for this book. It is particularly pleasing to include comments by long-serving UDC Clerk Ivo Nash, present Editor (and my successor) Tony White and that indefatigable apprehender of train robbers, Det Supt Malcolm Fewtrell.

But to end at the beginning, this book is largely the work of Arnold Baines, and that is as it should be for, in 1974, when I was researching Chesham's first proper history, I asked him to write it, he declined, but gave me invaluable advice and read my final draft; now it is my turn and pleasure to facilitate his work, with one difference — he needs no advice from me, for he is Chesham's historian, and twenty years later, he has at last been brought to book!

It anyone has been inadvertently omitted, I take responsiblity — final thanks go to the staff of Chesham Town Council, for their support, especially Irene Brown; the Library for facilities, the Record Office and District Council for access to the minute books, the Council for its active encouragement and the subscribers, without whom it would have been impractical — *EDITOR*

Steve James, the Mayor of Chesham in the Council's centenary year.

FOREWORD

by Councillor S. W. James, Town Mayor:

'All roads lead to Chesham!' This might not be strictly accurate but we can say that they are all downhill. In 1889 access was made even easier by the arrival of the railway, steam was here to stay, the world was changing quickly, and with it the town of Chesham. It was in this melting pot that the first elected Council was created, one hundred years ago.

As Mayor during this Centenary Year it is my pleasure, rather than duty, to introduce this history of the last 100 years of the people, places and community that make up the town of Chesham. I hope that the following pages of tales, history and photographs will trigger pleasurable memories of perhaps forgotten family, friends or events.

As you will see and read in this book, the pace of change during the last one hundred years has been rapid. Let me slightly amend a proverb — 'Nothing is certain but change and taxes'. There is no reason to believe that the pace of change will diminish and with the Town Council's motto — 'Serve One Another' we can continue together for many centuries yet to come.

20th century councillors who made their mark included these Chairmen of the District Council: F. E. Howard 1912-13, 1922-23, 1929-30, 1934-36; G. O. Bell 1938-47; A. P. Patterson 1928-29, 1932-33, 1937-38, 1953-54; Mrs F. K. Brandon 1957-58; W. T. Moulder 1956-57, 1959-60, 1964-65; Mrs K. L. Harries 1967-68, 1971-74.

INTRODUCTION

In 1894 Mr Gladstone was struggling with age, blindness, family tragedy and the House of Lords. Queen Victoria still regarded him as a dangerous old fanatic but, despite failing powers, he remained her Prime Minister just long enough to restore local democracy to the villages and smaller market-towns of England.

For most of the Victorian period, the attention of reforming Ministers and Parliaments had been concentrated on the great cities and especially on the hideous squalor of the new manufacturing towns. The age-long oligarchy of county government had at last been reformed, at least formally but, for most working people, the county town was too far away and daytime meetings inhibited their participation. For them the parish was the natural centre, where men (not to say women) could and should manage the affairs of their own community. The parish vestries and the manor courts were moribund, and they needed a new instrument of local government.

Their immediate demands were simple and basic. In the hamlets, labourers who emptied the contents of pail closets onto their gardens wanted main drainage and pure water. In the towns, workmen who already had these facilities were seeking allotments in 'garden fields', street lighting and paving, and places for their families to play and especially to swim.

In Chesham the tide of democracy was already rising. Among the voluntary institutions which were schools of self-government and mutual service were the chapels, the choirs and bands, the sporting clubs, the Co-operative movement, the Building Society, the Mechanics' Institute, the Temperance Society, the incipient trade unions and the friendly societies. Elective bodies with limited legal powers for special purposes already existed. There was a School Board which had taken over the schools founded by the churches; a Burial Board, the old churchyards being full; and especially the local Board of Health, replacing the poor law Guardians who still constituted the sanitary authority in the rural parishes. Under Mr Gladstone's Act, the possession of this Board entitled Great Chesham to an Urban District Council which could also act as the Parish Council.

Eighty years later, after a memorable campaign Chesham retained its Town Council. Now, once again, local government is in turmoil.

This book records and celebrates democracy in Chesham.

ABOVE: Ley Hill in the 1920s; Stone Age hand axes surfaced at the brickworks. BELOW: Latimer seventy years ago; Romans first farmed here.

ONE THOUSAND YEARS

Before the recorded history of Chesham began, the Chess Valley had many thousands of years of unrecorded activity, known only from surviving objects. Flint tools and pottery, even when broken, are not readily destroyed. Stone hand-axes found at the Ley Hill brickworks and in the footings of Cestreham School (now the Chesham campus of the College of Further Education) are solitary relics of hundreds of centuries of the Old Stone Age, during which the ice-sheet advanced and receded, but was held back by the Chiltern escarpment.

Ten thousand years ago, before Britain became an island, the climate was warming up for the present post-glacial or interglacial period. With the subsoil still frozen, the spring and summer rains scoured out what are now the dry coombes falling into the four main bottoms converging at Chesham. Tundra became woodland, and small bands of hunters and gatherers ventured up the Thames Valley and into the Chilterns. Six thousand years ago, during the Atlantic climatic phase, some of them made their base, at least seasonally, at Stratford's Yard off East Street, near where the streams unite to form the river Chess. Here these Middle Stone Age folk erected a structure, later covered by layers of downwash from Dungrove. They fashioned flint tools and hunted wild cattle, wild boar and red deer. Some small cattle bones suggest the beginning of farming. Hereabouts there is no clear distinction between the late Mesolithic and the early Neolithic (New Stone Age) period, when settlement became more permanent, forest clearance began and cereals were first grown. With agriculture came warfare; the dawn of the Bronze Age is represented by a bronze sword from Hawridge and a dagger from Lee Common.

The Chiltern Hills remained heavily wooded, and were still thinly peopled when Iron Age immigration began about 700 BC starting, it seems, with Ivinghoe Beacon. Tribal organisation developed and Celtic art and mythology flourished. Our area probably looked to the hill-fort at Cholesbury as seat of government, centre for trade and worship, and refuge in war. About 75 BC, only a generation before Julius Caesar landed in Kent and reached the Chilterns, Belgic adventurers made Cholesbury their headquarters. Their pottery is found alongside coarser ware in the Early Iron Age style; there was no immediate fusion of cultures.

No Iron Age site is known at Chesham but, during the uneasy peace after the Roman conquest, settlement moved downhill as the population increased, and a Romano-British village in the Wey Lane neighbourhood is evidenced from the first century. Following the last tribal revolt in 117, the Emperor Hadrian slighted the hill-forts and converted the Catuvellaunian aristocracy into city fathers of Verulamium, where St Alban was martyred in 209. Some tribal leaders were settled on estates along the Chess, each with about 500 acres of crops and grass, neatly spaced two Roman miles apart. The splendid villa at Latimer, which replaced a little Iron Age farm, flourished until near the end of Roman rule, and was succeeded by a farm during the fifth century. Its occupants were probably Germanic newcomers who leased the estate from an absentee landowner and undertook to render military service when needed. They knew how to construct timber crucks but had no use for stone and mortar. They hunted deer and practised free-ranging of cattle.

Usually villas and villages were incompatible, but Chesham had been settled before the imperial power imposed the villa system, and the humble community between Missenden Road and Germains probably outlasted the villa. On this gently rising ground south of the water-meadow, local archaeologists have found a rubbish pit and hundreds of broken jars, dishes and bowls, but hardly any coins and only one area of clay flooring, at Dawes Close.

One attraction of our neighbourhood was its chalybeate or iron-bearing springs, which later made the reputation of the local watercress and nearly made Chesham a spa. In the sixth or early seventh century, the really Dark Ages, Saxons from Middlesex followed the later-named Chess, then called the Isene from its iron-charged springs, until they came to the riverside meadow (the *hamm*) beside a collection of pudding-stones which they called a *ceastel*. Hence *Ceasteles-hamm*, the water-meadow by the stone-heap. They settled on the Nap in Church Street, between *ceastel* and *hamm*. Both still survive; recurrent floods (as in 1918) have inhibited permanent building in the meadow, and the great pudding-stones or breeding-stones are in the foundations of the Parish Church. The meeting of three streams would surely have been sacred, and there was a Bidwell where Ebenezer Cottages stand near Bury Lane. By coincidence, Ebenezer means 'stone of help'.

The Saxons subjugated the surviving Britons, who had lost their culture and soon lost their language. The field-name Cumbers in Herbert's Hole suggests that the invaders appropriated the better land nearer their settlement centre, *Cumbrium* — 'fellow-countrymen', a fairly polite term for natives.

Christian worship was maintained at Verulamium, where works of healing attributed to St Alban continued, and the Faith returned to our region through the ministry of St Birinus in the 640s. The Church placed the mysterious stones under the church of St Mary.

The villagers of Chesham ploughed the Town Field, held their folkmoots, sent their best men to the hundred moot at Burnham, and paid their dues to the King of Wessex or the King of Mercia, whichever was stronger. Around them stretched the Chiltern forest, a refuge for Britons and outlaws. The tide of clearance, westwards and northwards from the centre, can be traced by the diversification of the trees and shrubs in the hedges. Among the richest in species is the boundary between Captain's Wood and the Comps (an ancient field-name, still occasionally heard), but other valley-side edges of primary woods are also Saxon in date. Prevalence of bluebells is a good indicator of age. Expansion of the cultivated area accelerated in the tenth and eleventh centuries, but the daughter communities are not in the bottoms. Except for Waterside, they were established on the ridges, where exploitation of the heavier soils proceeded more gradually.

Chesham emerges into recorded history in 970, with the will of the Lady Ælfgifu, Latinized as Elgiva, whose marriage to her cousin King Edwy was annulled on dubious grounds by the Archbishop of Canterbury. Edwy died soon after, aged 19, and his brother King Edgar enlarged Elgiva's estates and made or confirmed to her a valuable grant of convicts condemned to penal slavery, whom she used effectively in the forest. By her will she liberated her slaves in the hamlets of Risborough (Loosley means 'pigsty-clearing') but apparently not those elsewhere. She left several of her Buckinghamshire manors to Edgar, and devised other lordships to various minsters, among them Chesham to Abingdon Abbey, probably through her devotion to St Ethelwold. A notable feat of civil engineering, the diversion of the Chess from Chesham Moor to give a good head of water at Lord's Mill, may have been due to Elgiva herself or to the Abbey, though Abingdon did not keep her gift for long. Edgar's death was followed by an anti-monastic reaction, and in the following century Chesham seems to have been at the disposal of the over-mighty Earl Godwin. His daughter Edith, wife of King Edward the Confessor, and her thegn Brihtric held estates in Chesham, while three sokemen of Brihtric and two others of Edith's brothers, Earl Harold (later King) and Leofwine (Lewin), held most of the rest. After the Norman Conquest the land of Brihtric and the earls' men was forfeit, but not Queen Edith's own; she transferred it to a Saxon whom the Norman scribes called 'Alsi' (Ælfsige or Æthelsige?). It was perhaps as a favour to Edith, if not previously to Elgiva, that Chesham was assessed to geld at about half its true value, making it, like Amersham, an 'enterprise zone'.

William was at Berkhamsted when the magnates of London submitted to him, none to soon, for his army was harrying the neighbourhood unmercifully. Some of it had hardly recovered twenty years later, when the Domesday Survey of 1086 gives us the first full description of the district. Brihtric's land, now held by Hugh de Bolebec, included Lord's Mill and most of the meadows, and his woodland, which supported 800 pigs, was charged with supplying iron ploughshares; this implies a local industry. Alsi had nearly all the rest of the woods, but the Bishop of Bayeux, King William's half-brother, had two of the four mills — Chesham was never again to enjoy the benefits or bear the burdens of a unified ownership. This helps to explain its variety of industries, its nonconformity and radicalism, and the fact that, unlike Amersham, it never became a borough.

The Normans could not pronounce the name, which by 1086 was something like Chestlesham. The nearest they could get to it was Tsestresham (written Cestresham) which became Cestreham, produced with initial *s*. The locals, who retained initial *ch* (unless they were Danes, who used *k* as in Kesters) began to drop the middle syllable in the 1240s, and by 1300 the name was written Chesham and pronounced Chessam. The name Chess for the river was formed from this, perhaps not before the early nineteenth century.

Brihtric's land, forming the principal manor, Chesham Higham, passed by marriage from the Bolebecs to the de Veres, Earls of Oxford. Hugh, the fourth Earl, held his court in 1264 in the Park, which was half a league round; a parker was appointed in 1321. In 1257 Earl Hugh was granted a Wednesday market and an annual fair of three days on 14-16 August, but in 1448 the Sunday Fairs Act required the Assumption (our patronal Feast) to be treated as a Sunday, and three days of the fair were transferred to 21 April (Cattle), 22 July (Cherry Fair) and 28 September ('Statty', the hiring Fair). There was also a cattle fair on 13 November. The Act of 1448 has now been repealed, but its effect remains.

It is likely that when Earl Hugh marked out the Market Square (not ambitiously) he also laid out the High Street by enclosing strips from a furlong in the common fields, in order to attract craftsmen and merchants to his new town. The oldest existing town house is however in Church Street, nos 54-56. St Mary's Church was repeatedly altered and enlarged.

The new market town met a real need though, even in 1538, when the registers begin, the population of the whole parish of Great Chesham could hardly have been more than a thousand. Outside the town, which extended from White Hill to what is now Hyatt's Yard, there were eight hamlets: Hundridge, Chartridge, Asheridge, Bellingdon, Ashley Green, Botley, Latimer and Waterside. With some 12,750 acres, the parish was among the largest in southern

England. In consequence, not only the town but also each hamlet eventually had its own officers — surveyors, overseers, constable and moordriver (in Latimer, lanedriver) — almost as if it were a parish, as several have since become.

The early Middle Ages saw continuing clearance of forest and scrub. The old word for cleared land, *leah*, stands alone in The Lee, Ley Hill and Lye Green, but is combined with a pioneer's name in Botley. Some settlements, like Chartridge (Cærda's ridge) had grown into lively villages. In contrast, Hundridge (hounds' ridge), which by 1200 was a village with a priest in charge of its own chapel, shrank to a manor-house with a few cottages. Bellingdon probably began in Chesham Vale (the second element is probably *dene*) and migrated uphill to Wykeridge. The boundaries of the hamets did not correspond to those of the manors; in particular, Chesham Higham and Chesham Bury held intermixed strips in the small open fields, so that separate manor courts could hardly have regulated the crop rotation.

From the early twelfth century until 1369, the Bury manor was held by the Sifrewast family, who gave Cannon Mill to the canons of Missenden Abbey and later granted them Wulfric the miller with all his progeny. This was witnessed by the whole hall-moot, c1166. These twelfth and thirteenth century charters are full of fascinating details. We meet Seric Puffa and Geoffrey Pug, as well as the families of Weedon, Broc, de Bois and Cheyne. We read of reeves and foresters, of disputes over sluices, of assarting in Pednor, of strange rents such as a rose or a pair of gloves, of twenty days' harvest work due (besides rent) from a virgate and a half — some 45 acres, about an average villein holding. Each common field and enclosed croft already had its name.

After many vicissitudes, including an escheat to the Crown, the Bury manor was acquired by the Earls of Oxford in 1490. They held it with Higham until 1579, when it passed to the Ashfields. The Earls also claimed the overlordship of Grove Manor in Whelpley Hill, but the Cheyne family held it under them from 1362. The Cheyne influence must have encouraged the local Lollards, the followers of Dr John Wycliffe, Master of Balliol, 'morning star of the Reformation'. Chesham Lollardy reached its climax with Thomas Harding, whose land was in Dungrove field. He was burnt at the stake in the dell at White Hill on 30 May 1532, after being knocked on the head. The details of his martyrdom became part of folk-tradition. Harding suffered for a principle on which all Christians now agree, the right of everyone to read the Holy Scriptures in their own language.

During the next hundred years, the population of Great Chesham doubled to 2,000. By 1605 St Mary's had a thousand communicants; 'the Seates and pewes were very fewe, and those decayed and broken and very uneasie and unfitt for persons of anie good sort to sitt in being confusedlye sett up with old broken bordes ... some of the meanest accompt had gotten the best seates'. The Vestry, or town's meeting, entrusted the Earl of Bedford's agent with a thorough restoration; the new galleries for young people lasted until 1869. The Ashfields wanted their tenants to sit together, but characteristically some people were unwilling 'to sitt as they were appointed'.

In 1555 Parliament made the Vestry responsible for highways; the parish was replacing the manors as local authority. Previously the manor court had dealt with overhanging hedges and other obstructions. The surveyors or waywardens in the town and each hamlet collected a rate for repairing the roads; this was quite distinct from the poor rate, levied by the overseers, and the county rate collected quarterly by the constables.

Of the craftsmen of Chesham, shoemakers were the most numerous; the tanners and curriers supplied leather to them and the glovers. Next came the wheelwrights, smiths and ploughwrights and the various workers in woodenware, described as turners, shovelmakers, trenchermakers and so on. They were just near enough to London to walk there to sell their wares. Then there were the millers, maltsters, potters (at the Emmanuel kilns) and tilemakers — at Tylers Hill this trade preceded brickmaking. The poundmaster or 'pinner' impounded stray cattle; there was another pound at Latimer. The 'sayer' or market assayer prevented unwholesome food from being sold. The making of Bucks Point lace and of straw-plait, 'the staple of Chesham', came rather later.

The most frequent surnames in the early seventeenth century were Birch, Weedon, Cocke, Gate, Dell, Gardner, Grover, Harding and Ware. The Puddephatts, known in Dacorum since 1225, began moving in about 1617. We miss some names which later became characteristic of Chesham: Gomm, Dwight, Brandon, Howard, Darvell, Reynolds and Bates. Reading, Batchelor and Hawkes have persisted throughout, and Barnes, Wright, Pearce, How, Mead, Webb and Hearn have increased. The Weedons have declined, but Thomas, son of Richard Weedon of Pednor, immortalized the name by his Almshouses, founded in 1624, in the Forelands of the Town Field for four poor godly people (now increased to eight).

Chesham has few medieval buildings, but many which date from the Great Rebuilding of the sixteenth and seventeenth centuries: the old Post Office (the 'Last Post'), the Golden Ball (Aureole House), the old Sun Lodging-house (removed to Pednor), many houses in Church Street, Germain Street and Pednormead End and various outlying farmhouses, as the open-field holdings were consolidated between c1480 and c1630, though there was no formal enclosure; cultivation in strips or 'slipes' persisted until the last century in the Bellingdon fields at both ends of Ramscote Lane. Cultivation terraces, notably the Balks, are a lasting relic of the system.

Chesham resisted Ship Money, took the Parliamentary side in the Civil War and was very Whiggish thereafter; after Waterloo Blucher was honoured, but not Wellington. The heirs of the Lollards became Baptists. The Broadway General Baptist Church was 'in a flourishing state' in 1676, despite the penal laws; it was closely linked with Berkhamsted and Tring, and was already distinguished for its sturdy orthodoxy. The two Sextons, grandfather and grandson, preached there for 111 years. In the twenty years after the Glorious Revolution and the Toleration Act, twenty houses in Great Chesham were licensed for worship. From these cottage meetings emerged the Lower Baptist Meeting (now Trinity) originally linked with Hemel Hempstead and Watford, and the Presbyterian (later Congregational, now United Reformed) Church, with its succession of learned ministers. In the eighteenth century the local Nonconformists prospered. John Ware became High Sheriff of Bucks, bought the great house in the Park from the last of the Whichcotes (who planted the original Avenue) and gave it to his daughter on her marriage with Coulson Skottowe, a notable benefactor of the Congregational Church.

The Lowndes family, who had completed the Bury by 1716, were social rivals of the Skottowes, and in 1798 bought and demolished their mansion; it had been the rectorial manor of Leicester Abbey, with its Lollard connections. One odd result of the early division of Chesham was that St Mary's had two vicars, one appointed by Leicester (St Mary de Pre), the other by Woburn Abbey. The livings were consolidated in 1767, when the Duke of Bedford built the present Rectory in the churchyard. The Woburn vicar seems previously to have lived on his glebe near the site of Thomas Harding School; the house there was let until it became too dilapidated, and then served as a tithe-barn. The Leicester vicar had lived at Mount Nugent. The rectorial estate of Chesham Woburn, extending from Germains to Hyde House, came into the hands of the Fullers.

The modern history of Chesham begins in 1845, with the formation of the Chesham Gas Company, the Chesham Building Society, now the oldest in the world, and the National School in Church Street, complementing and competing with the older British School in Townfield. By 1870, when education became compulsory, Chesham had provided places for 600 children by voluntary effort, but a School Board was still needed. In the fifteen years after 1845, new institutions were established almost every year: the Fire Brigade in Amy Lane, following some rick-burning; the Cricket Club; the County Court, later lost to Amersham; the Mechanics' Institute with its library; the first separate Infant School; the first Girls' School; the Temperance Hall; the first Savings Bank; the Cemetery; the Police Station; the Town Hall, largely rebuilt in 1856 by the first Lord Chesham (the Market House had served as Town Hall at least since 1679).

Until this period Chesham had been a town of individual craftsmen. The writer's great-grandparents, who made wooden spoons for Windsor Castle, were neither employers nor employees, and never worked outside their own house in Waterside. But by the 1860s Chesham was becoming a town of small industries, still based on craftsmanship, but inevitably involving tension between master and men, even though they spoke the same dialect and worshipped in the same chapels. Of the workshops of Waterside, some disappeared, some grew into factories, there or in Newtown. The boot manufacturers began to work for export. Steam power came into use at the mills. Beech woods were planted to meet expected demands.

As the population increased, so did overcrowding in the Yards. Chesham, which had been almost proverbially healthy in the seventeenth century, was swept by epidemics in the nineteenth. The last and worst was in 1871, when Dr Faithorn and three nurses gave their lives. The vicar, A. J. Aylward, a man greatly beloved, who had seen St Mary's restored and Christ Church built, worked unceasingly until he too died. The poor of Chesham erected his memorial.

Under the Public Health Act of 1875 the new Rural Sanitary Authority for the Amersham Poor Law Union provided main drainage to the sewage works opposite Milk Hall, soon followed by the Waterworks at Alma Road (for the urban area, not the villages). Nevertheless, the old dislike of control from Amersham soon revived. Chesham had rioted in 1454 to establish its parochial independence, and in 1835, less successfully, in defence of the poorhouse at Weylands, which was to be displaced by the Union Workhouse at Amersham (now a listed building, part of Amersham Hospital). Good government is no substitute for self-government, and in 1884 Chesham secured its own Local Board of Health, whose existence was the reason why Chesham was able in 1894 to replace both the Board and the Vestry by an Urban District Council. In this decade the drainage and waterworks were completed; Chesham Generals (ie General Baptist) Football Club began, rivalling Chesham Town Football Club; the railway arrived, and the paper

Mineral Cottage, focus of the 1820 chalybeate spa on the Moor, fell into disrepair — the ironspring stream, the Isene, attracted Saxon settlers.

which is now the *Bucks Examiner* started. The Third Reform Act widened the franchise (hence Franchise Street and Gladstone Road) and an elective County Council replaced the rule of the magistrates. After a hard fight, Mr Gladstone's last administration completed the elective structure of local government. It is a centenary well worth celebrating, and a heritage worth defending.

ABOVE: The Nap in Church Street ninety years ago, where the Saxons settled in the seventh century. BELOW: An unusual early view of St Mary's Church and the Vicarage, from the Park.

ABOVE: The Chess at Waterside, where Lord's Mill reflected the Lady Elgiva's slave labour, local estates and the engineering achievement which raised power and the foundation for the town's industrial heritage. BELOW: The Market Square was laid out in the 13th century — the 1679 Market House was replaced by the Town Hall in 1856. (SHF)

ABOVE: Older buildings like the Sun Lodging House in Church Street have not survived — here in 1937, before being moved to Pednor. (SHF)
BELOW: Broadway Baptist Chapel replaced an earlier building.

Aureole House — the Golden Ball — still represents the great rebuilding of the 16-17th centuries.

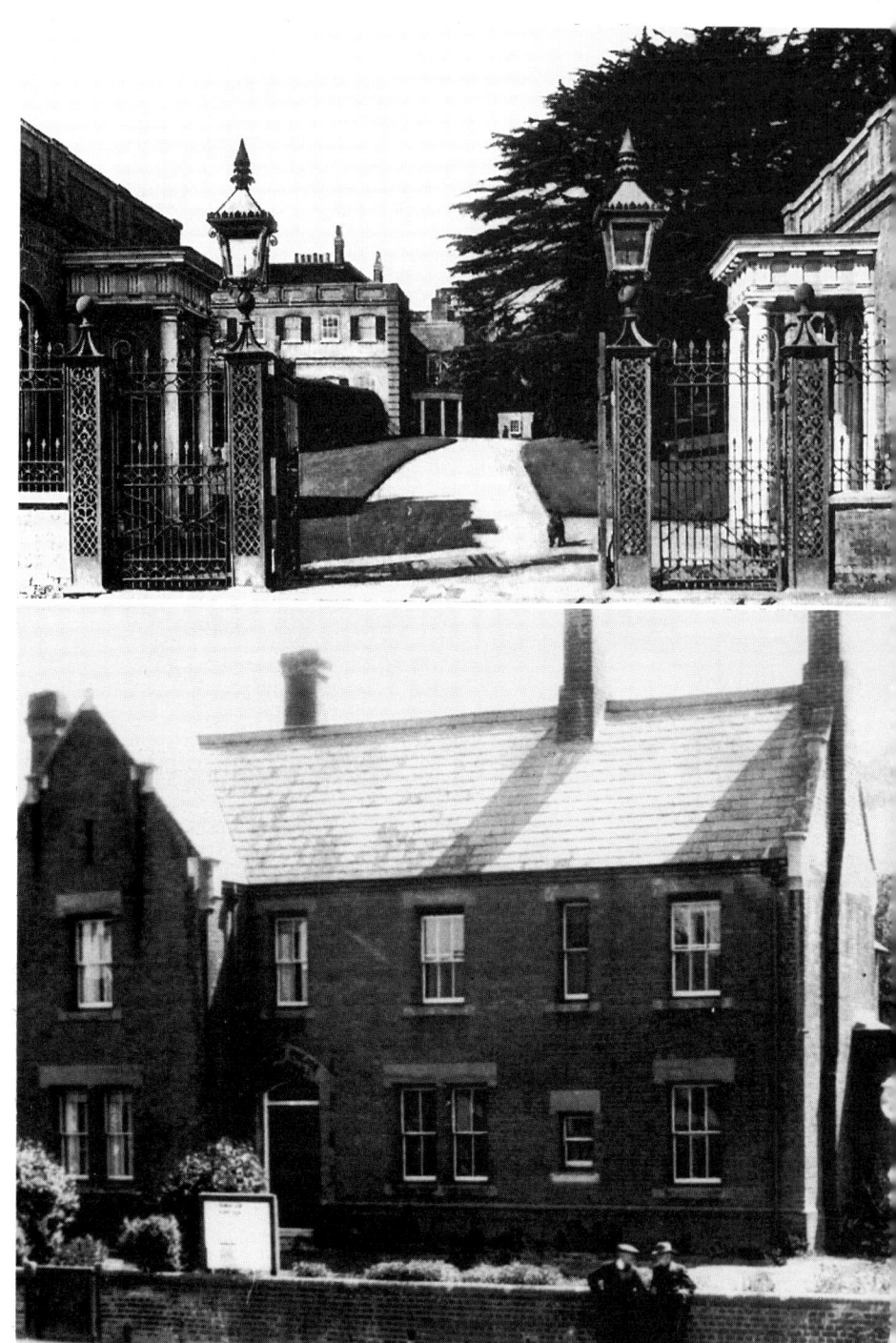

LEFT: Entrance to the Bury, 1716 home of the Lowndes family. BELOW: The original Police Station, built in the 19th century. ABOVE: The 19th century also saw the birth of the Fire Brigade. BELOW: Schools emerged, like Townsend Road Girls, here in 1897. (B)

25

ABOVE: Craftsmen formed the basis of Chesham's development, as workshops became factories; here Ted Elbourn works for Wright's and Jesse Moulder for East's — 20th century craftsmen in an older tradition. BELOW: Beechwoods were the basis for local industry which prospered into the second half of our century — despite occasional setbacks: Thos Wright's men ponder the soft going.

ABOVE: Steam power came to factory, farm and highway. BELOW: Water flowed towards the end of the century; this was possibly the engine shed a few years later.

Health hazards stemmed from Chesham's yards — like Lum's Yard, later Darsham Walk, here with the Star Yard car park gate open.

ABOVE: Christ Church in an early 20th century view — note the sluice on the Moor in the foreground. BELOW: The railways came, albeit terminating here; the goods yard was a busy place earlier this century.

ABOVE: Football flourished too: Chesham Generals, 1909-10 with left to right, back row: A. T. Stephenson (treasurer), E. Bateman, A. Thorn, F. Wright, A. Moulder, F. Dwight and W. Hawes (Chairman); centre: O. Orgill, S. Gomm, F. Newman (Captain), F. Mayo (Vice-Captain), F. Bone, W. Reynolds and bottom: W. Wilkins and W. Richardson. (LM) BELOW: The town the Council took over in 1894 was captured by Francis Frith within that same decade. The Bury is to the left of St Mary's, on the right just below the skyline.

Eighteen Ninety Four

On Wednesday, 19 December 1894, a sunny day with showers, the voters of Chesham, for the first time in our history, elected by ballot, in what was considered a thoroughly popular manner, a municipal governing body. For centuries the town's business had been conducted by the Parish Vestry, whose main secular concern was the relief of poverty. In 1835 this function was transferred to the Amersham Poor Law Union, which in turn begat the Amersham Rural Sanitary Authority and main drainage. The Parish felt strangulated, and in 1884 secured its own Local Board of Health. On the strength of this, Mr Gladstone's great Local Government Act gave Chesham an Urban District Council, the nearest thing to a Mayor and Corporation which the town could possess.

The Local Board had been elected by filling up papers at home, which were later open to public inspection. Now there was to be secret voting with a fairly wide franchise, including ratepaying householders, lodgers, and even some women ratepayers, though when husband and wife occupied property only the husband voted. Each elector had up to nine votes for the nine seats, but could give only one vote to a candidate. 'Plumping' or aggregating one's votes for one or two favourite candidates, as in School Board elections, was forbidden, but the old practice had some influence — the average number of votes cast by a voter was about five. There were only two polling stations, the new Board School at White Hill for the eastern side and the National School (now St Mary's Church Rooms) for the west. The villagers had to come in to vote. Twenty-four candidates stood, of whom eight issued addresses; four of these and six others had posters printed, while ten issued no address or bill. Three or four had horsedrawn vehicles bringing voters to the poll. Candidates stood on their personal merits, on which opinions were freely expressed. Great Chesham then had a population of about 8,440 of whom 1,449, or 17%, enjoyed the franchise. The turnout was 850, or 59%; this was then considered by no means heavy.

The ballot boxes were sealed at 8.00 pm, and held overnight at the National School. The count was completed at 2.00 pm and showed a tie for the ninth place, with two others only one vote behind. Mr Frederick How, Clerk of the outgoing Board, declined to use his casting vote as returning officer and directed a recount. The result, declared at 6.00 pm, was as follows:

Elected	*Votes*
Edwin Reynolds, boot and shoe manufacturer	393
William Lowndes, Esquire	279
George Barnes, boot and shoe manufacturer	234
Henry Catling, manager of the Co-operative Society	228
George Webb, brush manufacturer	225
Jesse Wright, woodenware manufacturer	198
Henry Butt, shoe manufacturer	192
Edwin Watts, junior, grocer	191
George Freeman, auctioneer and valuer	175
Not elected	
George Russell, brush manufacturer	174
Gaius Hawkins, assistant farmer	174
Charles Herbert, grocer	174
Thomas Turner de Fraine, farmer	163
Henry James Gibbons, architect and surveyor	162
Michael Seabrook, boot and shoe finisher	158
George Wallington, brushmaker	150
William Sibley, smith and wheelwright	147
Frederick Racklyeft, boot finisher	138
Henry Chilton, grocer	135
George James Smith, bookseller	114
James Woodley, general dealer	114
Gilbert Marshall, farmer	101
Henry Glenister Rose, grocer's assistant	77
Edwin Mead, tailor	68

The only survivors from the Local Board of Health were its Chairman, George Webb, and George Freeman, though only just. The Board's last meeting on Friday, 28 December, ended with testimonials and votes of thanks. The Council inherited its minute book, which remained in use, its seal, which was re-engraved, about £1,100 in hand (with no debts), two horses and twenty workmen, some of whom were paid ten shillings a week — less than the farmers paid, but they worked only three-quarters time, to give employment to more men. The steam roller was hired.

All the new Councillors came from the Town or Waterside. Five of the nine were masters in the traditional leather and woodenware industries; no farmers were elected. Jesse Wright entertained his employees, their wives and families at a numerous and happy Christmas party.

The new Council met at 5.00 pm on Wednesday, 2 January 1895 at the Mechanics' Institute, which then provided a library and reading room opposite the George Hotel. Edwin Reynolds, who had headed the poll, acted as temporary Chairman, with four on his right and four on his left. A tied vote for the Chair was expected, but George Freeman abstained (George Russell was still challenging the procedure of the count) so that Councillor Reynolds, proposed by Councillor Lowndes, was elected by four votes against three for George Webb, who then declined the Vice-Chair which was left unfilled. For twenty-five years Squire Lowndes of the Bury had chaired the Board of Guardians, who gave him an inscribed silver inkstand; he had provided land for the railway and White Hill School, and would have been elected Chairman had he not been a JP, but there was a strong demand for an additional Chesham magistrate, and the new Chairman was to serve *ex-officio* on the local bench.

The Council decided to meet at 6.00 pm and not to sit after 9.00 pm, except in case of emergency. A question time was introduced, as at Wycombe. Members discovered that they were not automatically a Parish Council, but could become one; thereupon they took steps to assume the powers and duties of a Parish Council, the powers of the Vestry, and the appointment of the Overseers. The School Board remained separate, and for the time being the Burial Board continued. Among live issues were the acquisition of the Moor from Lord Chesham; the adoption of the road from Tylers Hill Church to Ley Hill, said to be repairable by his Lordship (this has not yet happened); the improvement of unfit properties in the Yards, some of which had only one WC for three cottages; the registration of lodging-houses; street numbering and the revision of the Local Board's byelaws, some of which were considered ridiculous, but especially the promotion of a water undertaking. The Council set up five Committees, each with four members: General Purposes; Finance; Water and Lighting; Highways; Paving and Paths, which were said to have been shamefully neglected.

The electoral process and the absence of warding had effectively excluded seven of the eight hamlets of Great Chesham from the Council of the new Urban District, which they were soon to leave; but for the Town and Waterside a hundred years of initiatives for civic improvement had begun.

ABOVE: Most of the new Councillors came from the Town, typified in this 'Picturesque Bucks' postcard of a few years later. Star Yard (now the car park) is on the left and the cottages on the right were replaced by Brandon's — itself later split into various units. The Broadway was almost a pedestrian precinct. BELOW: The remaining councillors came from Waterside — where the Council's first duty concerned the Moor, and the Lord of the Manor's claim to rights over the river, pictured here in 1914. (SHF)

A CHESHAM CENTURY

1894-1902 The new Council lost no time in sending a delegation to wait upon Lord Chesham to secure the Moor so that it could be laid out as the recreation ground which Chesham, as a manufacturing town, greatly needed. It was cluttered with caravans and used for storing timber.

Lord Chesham conveyed all his rights in the Moor to the Council for £64 and his costs, but some of his copyhold tenants, led by Mr Garrett-Pegge and aided by the Commons Preservation Society, asserted their rights of pasture and opposed any unnecessary breaking-up, though they acknowledged the Council's statutory right to dig gravel for highway purposes.

In 1900 the Council realised the importance of the Commons Act just passed, and adopted a remarkably enlightened long-term programme: to drain and level the Moor, plant trees and shrubs; provide seats; construct a concrete wall to form the riverbank with path at side; make adequate provision for bathing; erect a rustic bridge over the stream; provide tennis, cricket and football pitches; improve the banks of the streams by camp sheeting; clear out the natural watercourses with a view to draining the boggy portion of the Moor, removing the weeds and sludge, planting water-cresses and generally improving and beautifying the Moor; bye-laws and regulations for the prevention of or protection from nuisances, or keeping order on the Common and its general management.

Within six months of the Council's establishment, there was a demand that the ecclesiastical parish of St John the Evangelist, Ashley Green, as defined in 1875, should become a distinct civil parish. The County Council made the necessary Order; the UDC petitioned the Local Government Board to disallow it, but too late, and the Order was confirmed in 1897. In 1900 Handpost Meadow at the foot of Nashleigh Hill was restored to Chesham (it is now occupied by housing and a prominent garage), but what was to become the 'Rec' remained outside the town boundary until 1934, though it had been rented by the UDC from the railway since 1922.

Chartridge and Latimer parishes were separated from Chesham in 1898. The Council did all in its power to extend the limits which were left when the ancient parish was cut up. These limits remained important even after the 1934 review, as they were still the bounds of the Town's water undertaking.

For the time being, the new parishes continued to use the Chesham cemetery. Ashley Green and Latimer made their own provision, but Chartridge has never had a burial ground. Chartridge Parish Council complained that to be charged higher fees was hard on the poor. Eventually, after litigation, an order of court in 1902 led to a Joint Burial Committee, to be convened initially by the Registrar of Burials, with ten members from Chesham and two from Chartridge. This continued until 1974, when Chartridge reverted to the arrangement under which their parishioners are buried here as of right, but at the strangers' rate.

The Council met in the large room at the Mechanics' Institute in High Street, called the Council Room. The membership was soon increased from 9 to 18, six retiring each year. The Council soon secured the powers of a Parish Council, with the right to appoint Assessors of Taxes, Overseers (originally overseers of the poor, they had become assessors of rates) and Constables of the Town and the eight Hamlets, whose theoretical duties were keeping watch and ward. Even after the villages seceded, part of each hamlet except Latimer was still within the Urban District. Indeed, there is a curious correspondence between the present wards of Chesham and the hamlets to which they look outwards from the town centre:

St Mary	Hundridge
Lowndes	Chartridge
Asheridge Vale	Asheridge
Pond Park	Bellingdon
Newtown } Hilltop	Ashley Green
Townsend/Codmore	Botley
Waterside	{ Waterside Latimer

Because the east side of the Berkhampstead Road was in the Hamlet of Ashley Green, though not in that Parish, the UDC appointed constables from that area for 'Ashley Green' until 1902, when the appointments were made only for the Town and Waterside.

In its early years, the Council was a somewhat contentious body, and recorded votes on corrections to the minutes were frequent. A standing order ('Rule 20') was adopted to restrain 'continued irrelevance, tedious repetition and unbecoming language'. In the last resort the Door Porter, who had a livery coat costing three guineas, could escort a disorderly member from the Chamber, but in 1901 his office was abolished. Next year ratepayers of Chesham were admitted to Council meetings; the doors opened a quarter of an hour early to admit the first 30.

The Council's biggest undertaking during its first decade was the High Level water supply, the 'Captain's Wood Scheme' (the Pond Park Estate is first mentioned in this context).

The villages suffered greatly in time of drought, and it was said that water in the district was much less plentiful than in former years. But outside the restricted area of the Urban District, provision had to be left to Rickmansworth and Uxbridge Valley Water Company and its Berkhamsted subsidiary — a private monopoly, as the Council complained. Indeed, it was only by the efforts of the Hon Walter Rothschild MP that a Bill to extend the Company's area to include Chesham was defeated on second reading.

The High Level scheme necessitated a frightening loan of £5,000 and then £1,000 more. The *Examiner* was accused by the majority in Council of unfairness in that only speeches opposing the loan were reported. But the result was to provide an ample supply of water for houses, factories and watercress beds; its ultimate disposal to the Company, when the Town would soon have lost it anyway, made the Elgiva Hall possible.

Main roads were maintained by the County, all other highways by the Urban District, but the Council took the initiative in improving Red Lion Corner, raising a mortgage on the Sewage Farm for this purpose. The roads were of flint, the footpaths mainly of gravel; paving and kerbing were gradually extended. The Council offered to gravel the Avenue through the Park, but William Lowndes preferred to do the work himself.

A major concern was making up private streets such as Station Road, Gladstone Road and Severalls Avenue, and the Council was a strong defender of rights of way, within and even outside the boundary. Seats were provided on Beech Tree Hill, the steep path from Townfield to Dungrove, and when these were vandalised they were reinstated.

Naming new streets, or renaming old ones, was often a matter of debate. The part of the Berkhampstead Road as far as the Sportsman was renamed Broad Street by 6 votes to 5, though the street numbering is still continuous. Chesham Bottom became Vale Road, but a request to rename Duck Alley as Riverside Terrace was not pursued. The extension of Eskdale Road to Codmore Cross was named Khartoum Avenue, but the name has not persisted. Essex Road replaced the developers' preference for Gordon Road, no doubt to avoid duplication.

Bathing on the Moor was probably an ancient custom, but its recorded history began in 1898 with an anonymous postcard to the Chairman (D. G. Patterson). Evidently the proximity of new houses at Shantung Place, Moor Road (known as 'China') led to complaints. It was agreed to abate the 'Bathing Nuisance' by erecting a dwarf concrete wall with a 6ft corrugated iron fence on top round the stream, provided that Mr Rose, the miller of Lord's Mill, allowed the sluice-water to be turned on in the evenings. The bathing place was to be 60ft by 35ft, with a wooden platform to dress on.

In 1902 it was decided to open the bathing place from 6 am until dusk on weekdays, with a man in charge who would collect a penny from each bather. From this small beginning the present swimming bath has developed.

From time to time the town suffered from epidemics of fever, when the schools and even the Sunday schools were closed. The Council built an 'Infectious Hospital' (Isolation Hospital) well along the Vale, by no means to the satisfaction of the Rural District Council. It was opened when it was needed. The Inspector of Nuisances was a busy man; the term Sanitary Inspector appears in 1902.

The Council regarded the Fairs in the streets as a nuisance, and asked the Home Secretary to abolish them. They seem not to have known of the Royal Charter. Local opposition to abolition was so strong that the Council first looked for another site, and then dropped the question.

An undue amount of time was devoted to initiating prosecutions for obscene language in the streets. Other offences included throwing stones, making slides in the streets and indecent scribblings. The Council strongly supported a Temperance Society initiative to prohibit the sale of intoxicants to children under 16.

The Council needed the Town Crier whenever the water had to be turned off, and provided a bell, but the Steward of the Manors claimed to make the appointment.

The Council was not too respectful of authority. A loyal address to Queen Victoria on her Diamond Jubilee was carried only by 5 to 3. The Council supported the South African war but not a war memorial for it, though as early as May 1900 it discussed 'what steps should be taken to celebrate the close of the war when it shall take place'. Peace Day was delayed for two years, and then the Council declined to pay for the Brass Band. Meanwhile, the return of a local hero, Major-General Lord Chesham, was welcomed.

The Council used local bricks rather than Leicestershire, and insisted on local Denner Hill stone setts for paving. (Examples of 'Denner Hilling' can still be seen, *eg* in King Street and Punch Bowl Lane).

1902-1918 The town had long had allotments in Bellingdon Road, beset by poultry, and the Duke of Bedford's Trust allotments were available for Waterside, but the demand was unsatisfied. Then in June 1909 Taylor's Farm came on to the market. The Council met the night before the auction and asked the Chairman (George Wallington) and two other members to bid for the whole farm, if possible; if not, for specified lots. They were successful, but were at

ABOVE: Chartridge was separated from Chesham in 1898 — about the time this picture was taken of Chartridge Green. (W) BELOW: Latimer left the new order too in 1898.

ABOVE: Chesham Waterworks was the pride of the Council — especially with the High Level scheme; inside the Higham Road works c1900. BELOW: Eskdale Road was extended to Codmore Cross, here in the 1930s, and called Khartoum Avenue — but not for long. OPPOSITE: Roads were renamed, but not Duck Alley, though this 1928 card uses the rejected Riverside name.

40

J. Lovering

Riverside, CHESHAM, BUCKS

ABOVE: Red Lion Corner was improved — in time for the emergent motorcar. BELOW: The Council supplied the fire engine.

personal risk if the Council could not secure a loan. The Local Government Board was not satisfied; in particular, they saw no need for the depôt which the Surveyor wished to locate in the farmyard, off what is now Cameron Road. The Board said sanction could not be given. The vendor threatened a writ against the successful bidders if the sale was not completed. They were in some danger, as the Council was divided 8 or 9 against 7 or 8 on the merits of the purchase. The majority agreed that the land should be conveyed to five named Councillors until the Council was in a position to take it over, and those Councillors who were willing executed a bond in favour of their colleagues.

Printed circulars were distributed to houses north of the Town Hall, and 200 ratepayers and others crowded into a meeting at the Townsend Road School. There was clearly a strong demand by the working classes for the proposed allotments, at rents varying from 3d to 9d a pole according to location.

On 25 February 1910 three Councillors with the Surveyor confronted officials at the Local Government Board, although a telegram had stated that the Board would rather have representations in writing. However, one officer conceded that the case looked different from that previously presented. The deputation proceeded to the House of Commons and enlisted the help of Lionel de Rothschild. On Monday the plutocrat MP for Mid-Bucks went to see the first working man to attain Cabinet rank, the Rt Hon John Burns, President of the Local Government Board. Burns called for a special report from his officers. When the Council met on Wednesday, the Chairman sent a prepaid reply wire to the Board. The reply telegram came on Friday; the purchase was sanctioned and the allotments were secured in time for cultivation to begin by Easter. Their administration was entrusted to the Highways Committee; a proposal to have a special Allotments Committee was declared not carried on a tied vote, and the present arrangement with tenant representation was not secured until 1953. To the Surveyor's disappointment the farmhouse and yard were sold off to Jesse Mead as a builders' yard, and the land adjoining Khartoum (now Eskdale) Avenue was also sold as surplus to requirements; it could have been let, and remains an orchard but at least the Council had 150 satisfied allotment holders, who soon formed a vigorous Association, which still invites the Town Mayor to present the trophies at its autumn show.

In 1909 the Council accepted the gift of a stone trough presented by the Metropolitan Drinking Fountain and Cattle Trough Association. It was installed in the Broadway, where the Town Pump had stood, and was soon used for unintended purposes. Not only cattle but traction engines were watered there; so were horses stabled in Station Road, to save laying on a supply to the stables. The trough, after a stay at the Pound, is now a flower bed in Lowndes Park.

In 1911 Dr Freeman Long, the Council's Medical Officer of Health, had his Annual Report printed at his own expense. It disclosed a manifest lack of suitable housing for working men. The Local Government Board took due notice, and drew the Council's attention to their powers under the Housing of the Working Classes Act, 1890. The reply was indignant: the Council had already invited offers from landowners, but had received none; members had viewed dwellings erected by other authorities, and found that they could not be made self-supporting unless rents of six shillings a week were charged. The Council would be competing with private speculators, who had secured permission for 60 cottages in Chesham during the preceding thirteen months. The Board were not satisfied, and in September 1912 the Council agreed to build twelve workmen's cottages. Meanwhile, cases of overcrowding and insanitary conditions were accumulating. A scheme prepared by a local architect found favour with the Council but not with the Board, and in 1913 architects and surveyors were invited to submit plans and estimates in line with the Board's sketch plans. The Council's own Surveyor, Percy Dormer, was successful, and the Brockhurst estate offered a 350 ft frontage at 30 shillings a foot. By this time the Council was pressing the Board to expedite the scheme. By June 1914 everything was settled, with a loan of £4,172 at 3½ per cent; most of this was for the main contract, repayable by 1974, but as regards the land, bought for £526, the loan was extended to 1994, which is thus another significant anniversary. The Council had reluctantly accepted Peterborough Fletton bricks rather than Bucks Calverts. The first tenants, at five shillings a week, were working-class people living in Chesham, mostly with old Chesham names, including Rance (twice), Mayo, Hawkes, Medley, Geary, Webb, Reynolds, Woodstock, Pearce and King, though there was also Sabatini. This Edwardian terrace has lasted well, and is now vested in the Chiltern Hundreds Housing Association. No doubt Dormer would have built more dwellings like them, but the Great War had already started.

The Council had been naturally and legitimately reluctant to use even its closing powers, and before 1913 it seems never to have made a demolition order; even the King Street cottages were eventually reprieved and repaired.

The Surveyor was also the Waterworks Engineer, and in 1906 a breakdown of the pumping plant might have proved disastrous for the town but for his energy and skill. He worked day and night, and the town was without water for only 38 hours. He received a resolution of thanks under the Council's seal. In 1909 he took over the duties of Water Inspector from the Inspector of Nuisances, but by then his main preoccupation was to reconstruct the sewers and improve the standard of the effluent. The Thames Conservancy was increasingly concerned at the pollution of the Chess. The enlargement of the sewage works was the Council's most expensive capital project, but it occupies little space in the Council records because it was obviously necessary and therefore not contentious; but when the Council decided to place a commemorative plaque on the new Swimming Baths they ordered another for the sewage farm.

The 1900 proposals for regulating and improving the Moor were long delayed, mainly because the Council had not acquired the river and the water rights. In 1904 the fence round the bathing-place was taken down to the level of the concrete wall, and in 1908 the Council resolved by 7 votes to 5 to revive the proposal for a Commons Act Scheme. Lord Chesham was asked to secure the Council's ownership of the 'small rivulets', and the Board of Agriculture and Fisheries approved their inclusion in a draft scheme, but advised that the small strip which was then in Chesham Bois parish should be excluded. The Council tried to reach agreement with objectors, but meanwhile there was a growing demand for a swimming bath, not necessarily on the Moor. A proposal for a site at the north end of Skottowe's Pond was advocated but was soon abandoned in favour of a site on the Upper Moor, and on 22 May 1912 a scheme for a bath 90 ft by 40 ft, three to five feet deep, was approved. The bath was completed and opened, with its commemorative tablet, although the owner of Lord's Mill, already in dispute with the Council, questioned their power to enclose common land for this purpose without the sanction of a scheme of regulation. Meanwhile expensive litigation on the water rights continued, and was not finally compromised until October 1913, under threat of exemplary damages. The Council acquired the bed of the Chess, from the railway bridge to 50 yards below the Mill, along with the backwater from the sluice, but the flow at Lord's Mill was safeguarded, as was the right to repair or re-erect the Mill, In fact, the new facility no longer depended on the river, as the water was pumped from a well, and the Council could turn more happily to new bye-laws, opening hours and season tickets. There were to be special sessions for gentlemen and ladies, first-class and second-class; the attendants were a married couple.

In 1903 the Joint Burial Committee agreed to let the cemetery lodge in Berkhampstead Road to the Urban District Council for use as the Surveyor's office and for committee meetings, but it was not suitable for meetings of the Council, and from 1909 these were held in the Town Hall, usually upstairs; thereafter 'Council Room' has this meaning, though meetings were held downstairs in the 'Corn Exchange' when the upper room was needed by the magistrates. Henceforward the public had free admission to Council meetings.

The Town Hall also accommodated the Fire Brigade until it moved to the upper High Street, and the Council paid for better lighting of the Fire Station and the Market House clock, but the whole building, however described, still belonged to the Lord of the Manor, whose consent was needed in 1914 for the installation of a Roll of Honour listing those serving in the forces from Chesham and adjoining parishes.

The duties of four full-time officers of the Council were set out in detail in 1910. They were the Surveyor and Waterworks Engineer (£220 a year), the Financial Clerk and Rate Collector (£85 rising to £104), the Inspector of Nuisances (£65 rising to £80) and the Roads Foreman (25 shillings a week).

The Fire Brigade's relationship to the Council was somewhat uneasy. The Council approved its officers, made an annual payment and supplied its appliances and equipment, including the steam fire engine, and could restrict their use outside the Urban District. However, the Brigade managed its own affairs, received subscriptions and made claims on insurance companies. A cheque sent by one such company direct to the Council was returned. Until 1911 each of the four adjoining parishes made an annual payment to the Fire Brigade as a kind of retaining fee. The Brigade used the town's coat of arms, but this was in any case unofficial until the grant of arms in 1961.

In the Council's earlier years no major highway works were undertaken or even envisaged. The most recent such improvement was the Amersham Road, constructed almost a century before, and this was still thought of as New Road. On the main roads, granite replaced flints. Paving and tarring proceeded gradually, and the making up of private streets proceeded *pari passu* with building development. When the Council sought to move faster than this, the Justices restrained them, and this issue seems to have occasioned the first Chesham Ratepayers' Association in 1907. In Khartoum (Eskdale) Avenue the Surveyor was instructed to plant trees when making it up. At the Council's instance, the combined Eskdale Avenue became a main road. There were a few name changes; it was decided to re-name Chartridge Lane as Park Road, but the old name has persisted for the part of the road not then built up. Hearn's Yard, which had figured too often in public health reports, became

Bury Lane. When there was distress in the town, the Council tried to expedite minor highway improvements to find work for the unemployed. In 1913 the Council demanded speed limits to avert the 'great nuisance and danger caused by the reckless driving of motor cars', and proceeded to buy a new horse to replace the Council's old brown mare.

The Council became increasingly concerned with external affairs. In 1908 General Booth of the Salvation Army received an address of welcome. Town's meetings were convened more often; in 1911 one supported Sir Edward Gray's proposals for international arbitration, and another initiated celebrations for the coronation of King George V, though the Council declined to underwrite the deficit.

Councillors' attitudes to what is now called subsidiarity were ambiguous. On the one hand, they were disinclined to accept delegation of Shops Act powers; on the other, they asked the County Council to entrust to Managers a larger share of control of the schools, and they considered that Governors of the Grammar School should be nominated by the parishes as well as the two District Councils.

In 1914, Labour almost swept the board at the spring elections. The Council had already conceded the unions' demand for a Fair Wages Clause in contracts for construction work. The Council, the unions and the traders joined in securing a workmen's train at cheap rates. The Council demanded that the County Council should provide school meals, and should change the election day to Saturday when workmen had a half-holiday. The Daylight Saving proposal for 'summer time' was endorsed, and the Council came within a casting vote of supporting women's suffrage. They stirred up the sleepy local charities, and began to look for a new Town Hall, Council Chamber and Council offices. A motion was tabled to secure a minimum wage of a pound a week. Then the war came.

The impact of the war on Chesham was not sudden, except that public houses closed at 8.30 pm. The Council's first thoughts were that projects would be needed to relieve distress, and that soldiers could well be billeted here, which the Army declined; but the King's Royal Rifles were played into Chesham by the town band, and were offered beer at the Town Hall or the Skating Rink as an alternative to sandwiches and soft drinks at the various Sunday Schools. The Council placed no obstacle in the way of men enlisting or engaging in armament work. But a year after the declaration of war, the demand was for postponement of works and strict economy. As regards the lighting programme, the Council thought that this

ABOVE: Taylor's Farm came on the market in 1909 – ideal for allotments, but some land, next to Khartoum (now Eskdale) Avenue, was sold off – it is still an orchard, behind the houses on the right, here in 1919. LEFT: In 1909 this stone trough replaced the Town Pump in the Broadway. RIGHT: It later went to the Pound, before becoming a flowerbed in the Park.

LEFT: The Town Hall hosted the Council's meeting from 1909.
RIGHT: Relations with the Fire Brigade were somewhat uneasy, though the gentlemen themselves seem fairly relaxed. BELOW: In 1906 the Park belonged to Squire Lowndes.

ABOVE: Sewage was the Council's main expense; the authorities worried about pollution in the Chess — here at Town Bridge in the thirties. BELOW: The town turned out for high days and holidays, like this National and Sunday Schools Parade down High Street.

would just curtail expansion, but soon street lighting had to cease, except for pilot lights. Refuse collection was reduced from twice to once a week, and insistence on proper dustbins was deferred. The Baths were opened only from Thursday to Sunday, and the ladies had to share sessions with the children. Henry Byrne remained Chairman throughout.

A Food Control Committee was set up with twelve members; there were murmurs that eight of these were members of the Co-op. No traders were included, and only one lady. Temporary allotments were secured; the Council bought seed potatoes for sale, encouraged the keeping of rabbits, pigs and poultry, and supported an Infant Welfare Centre, which got milk into babies, but they declined to distribute sugar for preserving soft fruit.

Difficulties increased during the last year of the war. The town's drainage system was damaged by a flood caused by a cloudburst. In July the indefatigable Surveyor became Fuel Overseer. He was also working on plans to permit early post-war housing development in Newtown, where the Council had secured an option to buy land, several times renewed. He died suddenly, two months after the Armistice, after twenty years of whole-hearted service. The Council placed a framed photograph in the Council Room.

1918-1939 Street lighting in Chesham was half restored a fortnight after the Armistice, but not fully for another year. Fuel and Lighting Committees were at an end, but a Profiteering Tribunal was still needed. The War Office presented Chesham with a German gun on its carriage; it was painted and remained in the Council's yard until 1927, when it was disposed of. The sacrifices made by the town and the nation were more worthily commemorated by the War Memorial in the Broadway, commissioned by a town's meeting, paid for by public subscription, and entrusted to the Council under the watchful eye of the British Legion. In 1927 it was protected by posts and chains. Each year the Armistice had a double commemoration; the silence at 11 am on 11 November and the memorial services on Remembrance Sunday.

Captain Hinchcliffe became Surveyor in July 1920. Thanks to his predecessors, fourteen houses on the Brockhurst estate were already under construction, and he secured the Housing Commissioner's approval for 89 more. The building byelaws were revised, although members claimed that they were not antiquated. The Surveyor sketched plans for an inner relief road, which members found excessively expensive; but the idea kept coming back until it was realised by St Mary's Way, for whenever the High Street was closed for repair the Park Avenue had to serve as a by-pass. In 1924 six dwellings were built in Severalls Avenue, and 25 near Cannon Mill for Waterside; but a major new site was needed.

ABOVE: Traffic was not an Edwardian problem in Broad Street.
BELOW: The Kings Royal Rifles marched into town in 1914. It was a wet day.

ABOVE: The Gallipoli gun was presented by the Rothschilds to the Royal Bucks Hussars — here at the Long family stables in Bellingdon Road, later Gilbert's Taxis. BELOW: This view from Dungrove was used for wartime postcards here in 1916.

The Council identified one in Asheridge Bottom, and eventually secured a compulsory purchase order in February 1927. At that moment 42 acres on the adjoining hill, known as Pond Park, were offered for £4,000. The Council forthwith accepted, relinquished Asheridge Vale for other uses, applied for a loan sanction and advertised for applicants for up to 150 houses — all this within a week. Councillor F. E. Howard, the estate agent, was later called 'father of Pond Park'. Once the land was off his books, he was free to expedite the first hundred houses — 25 parlour type, 50 non-parlour and 25 with two bedrooms. Albert Clarke was engaged as architect. Within a month he had an office on the site; a fortnight later he produced plans for a layout, with full plans a month later.

Meanwhile the Surveyor was in trouble. The Thames Conservancy stated that the Chesham Sewage Farm was the worst in the 4,000 square miles of their area. He was relieved of his sewage duties and resigned. The new Surveyor was the vigorous Frank Moss. A tender for Pond Park was accepted, though the Ministry of Health considered it low. The partnership collapsed in November, the second lowest tenderer could not produce a bond, and the third resumed work in February 1928. The tenants selected for Lansdowne, Manor, Highfield, Lyndhurst and Nightingale Roads were notified by August and, although their names were not read out, as had been usual, the first was Councillor William Moulder, who for another generation made Pond Park as well as the town's allotments his special care. His first complaint was that motor cycling clubs were using Pond Park Road as a testing hill.

The Council wished to commission sixty more houses, but could only proceed immediately with twelve, for which there were 54 applicants, but 12 of these were single men; of the rest, 14 were in lodgings and 28 in rented houses. The third phase, with thirty houses, gave us Overdale Road.

Although the Council had built 250 houses in the ten years since the war, there had been no real progress in improving housing conditions in the Old Town. It had long been a traditional status symbol in Chesham to own or buy cottages and to let them at low customary rents, but hardly to repair them. As the Council had not made closing orders, any which fell vacant were simply relet as they stood. When repairs were ordered at Chequers Yard, off Market Square, the owner served counter-notices which gave rise to deemed closing orders requiring the Council to rehouse his tenants.

In May 1930 the Architect was asked to take a month's notice on full salary, and was given a testimonial under the Council's seal and a £50 bonus. He resigned before the month expired and died a few months later. The Surveyor was appointed architect for the next fifty houses (Upland Avenue) with a full-time clerk of works. At the audit, the Council was surcharged, although the Architect had worked long hours, seven days a week, and had ensured early completion, securing an economy far greater than his bonus. The Minister of Health remitted the surcharge, but the Clerk, G. S. Scott, who had been implicated, had died suddenly the week before.

During 1931, Ministers were seeking economies, and until Pond Park was built up they were unlikely to sanction the purchase of land in the south of the town, from which so much of the demand came. Nevertheless in January 1932 the Council designated a clearance area comprising Townfield Yard and Stratford's Yard. In the year during which the compulsory purchase order was taking its course through the corridors of Whitehall, the Council started 24 more houses in Pond Park and rejected an offer by a private company to take over all the Council's housing. The Ministry deleted Stratford's Yard from the order (it was later demolished anyway) and excluded the Old British School and the cottage in White Lion Yard, which survive. Before the order became operative, Ministers had ended housing subsidies to local authorities except for slum clearance. The Council asked the Government to reinstate them, in view of overcrowding and the pressing need, and the failure of private enterprise to build houses for letting to the working classes at reasonable rents. Meanwhile they commissioned thirty more houses at Pond Park, with the Surveyor as architect.

In 1935 the Council took the critical decision to concentrate its programme of slum clearance into one stage. Instead of proceeding house by house, eleven clearance areas were designated in the Old Town and Waterside with 68 houses and 152 residents to be displaced. Some of these areas, such as Parsonage Lane, would have been lost anyway, but some, such as Duck Alley, would have been treasured in our time had they survived; once demolition orders were in operation, apparently they could not be rescinded. The result was to justify 100 more houses on the slopes of Pond Park, of which not more than 40 were for general needs and thus unsubsidised. The resulting new roads were named after poets who had lived in Bucks: Milton Road, Cowper Road and Chesterton Close. G.K.C. had died so recently that his name was referred back on the casting vote. Some Councillors wished instead to honour Gray, Burke, Harding or even Burns, but the Housing Committee stood its ground and prevailed.

Councillors were mindful of the need for social facilities on the new estate where so many Chesham families looked back towards their old houses. Areas for recreation were reserved; two members presented swings and another well-wisher a see-saw. A 'bus service was started and discontinued; its resumption by diverting the Tring 'bus was vetoed by the Traffic Commissioner because the hills were too steep. The Congregational Church was allowed the use of a surviving cowshed, from which the Hivings Park Free Church can claim indirect descent; a site was leased for an Anglican building, and the first steps were taken to establish a social centre. A public-house was precluded by a covenant in the conveyance to the Council.

The Housing Committee had Townfield Yard, but with no clear mandate what to do with it. Suggestions included a car park, a new Market Square and a swimming bath. On 24 February 1937 the Chairman of the Committee demanded clear instructions so as not to waste any more time. The decision, eventually unanimous, was for 'a Model Village of residences for old people'. This purpose was achieved in 1938, with the name Townfield retained (not Yard or Close) and with a commemorative stone tablet. Next year the Council bought the burnt-out factory, once the Townfield Baptist Chapel, where the warden's flat now stands. The old burial ground could not be obtained; it now serves Trinity Baptist Church.

Although no one but the Council would build houses for letting, most of the Urban District was available for development by speculators. In 1925 a road was made from Bellingdon Road up to Chartridge Lane; at first called Breda Avenue, it was renamed Lowndes Avenue with that family's consent. Penn and Hampden Avenues followed. 'Racklyeft's Estate' occurs in 1930; the names of Belmont and Ridgeway Roads were bestowed some three years later, but the Council had already ensured that they were sewered, with no concession for existing cesspits, and that Ridgeway Road had street lighting. The adoption of these roads was so strongly opposed that the procedure fell into abeyance on the outbreak of war and has not yet been resumed; hence the oddity that the Town Council still pays for footway lighting in this private road. Woodley Hill (so named instead of Unicorn Hill, on a casting vote) is the only other such anomaly.

There was an outbreak of estate development in 1937. The Hilltop Company proposed to build 336 houses within 18 months, and made a start on Manor Way, in such haste that the footings of one house were being dug across a public footpath until the Surveyor intervened. However, by the end of 1938 the Hilltop developers were in liquidation and work on many uncompleted houses had stopped.

The Chessmount estate was under way by June 1938, and the names of Chessmount Rise and Fryer Close were approved two days before the war. The Great Hivings estate had not begun.

Development just started at Mapletree Farm precipitated the first move to protect woodland; it would have entailed widening Tylers Hill Road and making up Bottom Lane, perhaps all the way down to Milk Hall in Latimer Bottom, but from this and other prospects Chesham was delivered.

The High Street was the only way through Chesham, and there was a bottleneck at its southern entrance. The Council promoted the widening of Red Lion Street. The Ministry demanded a 45 foot width, extending into Amersham Road, and after a public inquiry made a Provisional Order subject to confirmation by Parliament. Our local Act received Royal Assent on 10 July 1930, but this was only the start. Notice to Treat followed, and it was not until 1934 that agreement was reached with Mr Garrett-Pegge on how much of his land should be acquired. The surplus became the Red Lion Street Gardens. Work finally proceeded in 1937. One result was the rebuilding of the Red Lion, which took over the licence of the demolished Nag's Head. The Pound was dedicated as part of the highway.

Inevitably, the widening concentrated attention on the Town Hall. The Council met there and resolved that its demolition was so desirable that they would buy it. A week later they rescinded this as too hasty, and asked the County Council to acquire it as a highway improvement. The County replied that it was really a town improvement, but they would share the net cost. The Ministry disagreed, and the two authorities then put the proposal into their Town Planning scheme, as an improvement to the Market Square and Church Street. This went to public inquiry in May 1939, but by then the Town Hall was needed as a training centre for air raid precautions, and once again the war deferred a decision.

The growth of traffic had other consequences. The opening of the Star Yard car park in 1938 on land acquired for slum clearance at last alleviated the choking of the town centre by parked cars, and allowed the Broadway to be rearranged. Pedestrian crossings had been introduced in 1934.

In 1920 the Council leased the lower part of the Park from Mr W. F. Lowndes as a public recreation ground. They took early action to prohibit fishing in Skottowe's Pond, to put a concrete edge around it, to create and plant an island in it, to provide seats and to adopt byelaws. The Silver Prize Band played in the 'Circle' and two boats were placed on the lake. Mr Lowndes' consent was sought to repair the roadway and gates, but he regarded topping the trees as a matter for Councillors, who were anxious not to destroy their beauty. The first commemorative tree in the Park was a copper beech planted by the White Hill senior girls in 1925. That winter skating was allowed, at a charge of twopence (under 12, a penny; free on Sundays).

Councillor Ralph Howard asked for a pottle of maize to be bought for feeding the swans. The island, being artificial, was liable to be washed away; a decision to protect its sides by camp sheeting was 'held over' at the time of the General Strike, but elm boards were placed in 1932. A 'sand dump' for children was provided in 1928, and there must have been swings, since objection was taken to their use on Sundays. As late as 1932 religious services in the Park were held to be beyond the terms of the lease, so that the Salvation Army could play but not preach or pray, but in 1937 the minister of Hinton was allowed to hold a service on Whit Sunday. The fish had multiplied, and in 1932 fishing was allowed at F. G. Plummer's instance, a decision reversed five years later. The surplus from the town's Silver Jubilee celebrations was used to provide a shelter in time for Coronation Day, and the local memorial to King George V took the form of children's play equipment; the slide was inaugurated by propelling the Chairman down it. Squire Lowndes provided a more lasting memorial, an extension of the lower Park, also opened that day. The Local Education Authority was already seeking to relocate the girls' school in the upper Park, on the level, and three-way negotiations ensued, in which the Council sought to purchase the freehold reversion of their lease and to acquire whatever part of the Park the County Council did not need; these discussions were interrupted by the war.

The scheme for regulating the Moor, proposed as soon as the Commons Act 1899 was passed, was drafted and advertised in 1909, revived in 1922 when riparian objections had been resolved, and finally operative on 31 January 1924. Byelaws were made in 1925; next year Henry Rose celebrated his Chairmanship and realised a lifetime's wish by planting trees along the riverside. 'Kitty's Bridge' over the Chess near the sluice had already been opened. One important long-term decision taken in 1923, anticipating the Scheme, was to use the domestic refuse of the town to level up the swampy Lower Moor. Other refuse was tolerated and even welcomed at the 'Dust Shoot' or 'Dump'. The Amersham RDC, whose area impinged on the Moor until 1934, had to be assured that there were no rats there; but there were constant fires, started by mischievous boys.

The Scheme had virtually taken the swimming bath out of the common, and further changing boxes were provided. One hopeful petition asked that the baths be heated all the year round. Another objected to tennis on the Moor.

The alternations of the Fair between the Broadway, the Moor and even Nashleigh Recreation Ground hardly merit a record. The Council was not clear what standing it had in this franchise, once the Home Secretary had declined in 1923 to abolish the Fairs, which then still included cattle sales.

Nashleigh Recreation Ground had been bought for the Metropolitan Railway in 1890 and was the property of the Metropolitan and Great Central Joint Committee. Although it was then outside the Urban District boundary, it was leased to the Council for five years from September 1922 and thereafter on a quarterly tenancy. Despite this, the Council made byelaws, planted trees for shade and surfaced an area for children to play in wet weather.

The Cemetery can rank as a valuable open space. At Dr Long's instance, a large extension in Honeysuckle Field was secured by the Joint Burial Committee in 1921 and forthwith laid out. Although the town has since doubled in population, their foresight has provided for the whole century and probably for most of the next.

A long contest between Lord Chesham and the Council began in 1919, when he said that tarring the roads endangered his fish. Miss Dell's watercress beds were already suffering; her action succeeded at first instance and on appeal. The roads could only be patched until tar was replaced by tarmac and then by bitumastic. But it was soon realised that the main risk was from defective drains, and especially faulty old private connections. The town stream had mostly been culverted, but the culvert was falling in under the Broadway and elsewhere, and at least five outlets were discharging oil into it. Successive remedial projects financed by loans had only partial success, but in 1932 a new borehole 250 feet deep gave Chesham a secure water supply of the highest bacterial purity. Previously cesspits and soakaways near the water supply had constituted a serious risk; the overflow from the old borehole at the waterworks had always gone into the sewer. The Thames Conservancy were placated by an undertaking to comply with their standards, but Lord Chesham found that the Public Health Act of 1875 implied a higher standard, and in 1935 the High Court agreed. The Council wisely decided not to appeal; agreed damages were £3,000, but costs had mounted to £13,596. This was one reason for the Ratepayers' Association success in that year's election. Their leader, Geoffrey Bell, earned acclamations for convincing the UDC's Association conference that the law was impossibly stringent; but only new legislation could counteract the effect of the judgement.

The level of subsoil water varied widely. In 1934 Skottowe's Pond was nearly empty, and after a vain attempt to top it up the mud was cleared out. Yet by 1937 heavy rainfall had turned Chesham Vale into a watercourse (as in 1928 and often previously) and the road surface was washed away. As all the sewers were surcharged, surplus waste had to be turned on to a meadow above Weir House Mill, rented for the purpose. Lord Chesham had restocked his river, but he was forebearing, as a new relief sewer had already been commissioned.

Chesham and its Council had never quite accepted the loss of the hamlets, and Chesham Bois, the second manor of Chesham in Domesday, declared its ancient connection by its name. In 1928 an amalgamation with Chesham Bois was proposed as part of a reconstitution of Great Chesham. Perhaps even Hawridge and Cholesbury at the head of the Chess Valley could be brought in, though they had never been in the Chiltern Hundreds. Ralph Howard, now a County Alderman, used his best endeavours to persuade the parishes of the advantages of Chesham's services. Latimer was the most receptive, but they all demanded differential rating. During the general review of County Districts the Inspector patiently sought for an agreed solution, but Chesham found the final compromise disappointing, though the area of the Urban District was increased from 1,386 to 3,489 acres as from 1 April 1934, a year still to be seen on the boundary posts then erected on the roads entering Chesham. Lye Green came in, but Ley Hill remained in Latimer parish and Botley was divided, but the main change was the inclusion of Lower Bois, which is almost a part of Waterside and shares the Moor.

There were few procedural and no structural changes in the Council in the twenties and thirties. The Vice-Chairman was always the immediate past Chairman, if available. Recorded votes became fewer, and until 1935 membership had tended to stabilise, regardless of affiliation. Town's meetings were convened only for special reasons; for example, the Council now took responsibility for organising and financing the Coronation celebrations, though it sought co-operation with the townspeople at a meeting to be called when the 'present state of affairs' (the Abdication crisis) disclosed which King was to be crowned.

The Overseers disappeared in 1927; thereafter the Magistrates' precept requiring the appointment of Petty Constables was directed to the Council as their corporate successors, until in 1934 a resolution of Quarter Sessions declared Parish Constables no longer necessary in Chesham (they continued in Chesham Bois).

ABOVE: The Broadway immediately after the Great War — with restored public lighting. BELOW: The first War Memorial was erected in Market Square, a temporary edifice; the soldier was bought by public subscription and erected in the Broadway in 1921.

LEFT: It was later protected by posts and chains — in 1927. RIGHT: The Memorial without its chains. BELOW: Down came the old Red Lion for highway improvement, a year after this picture was taken. (SHF)

ABOVE: The new Red Lion took over the Nag's Head licence — demolished that same year, in London Road. (SHF) BELOW: The Royal and Ancient Order of Buffaloes raised funds for good causes, here in 1925 in Brockhurst Road. (MB)

ABOVE: Breda Avenue was renamed Lowndes. BELOW: The Broadway was rearranged with slum clearance at Star Yard. This aerial shot shows Broadway and High Street, Broad Street and Berkhampstead Road, in the 1940s.

ABOVE: The Generals played football on land between Severalls Avenue and Brockhurst Road until the 1920s. BELOW: Two boats were put on Skottowe's Pond when the Council leased the Lower Park — in 1920.

ABOVE: The unattended boats were easy prey for young lads; the buildings were demolished in 1959, and BELOW: skating was allowed at twopence a time, free on Sundays.

ABOVE: Councillor F. E. Howard served as Chairman for five terms, 1912-13, 1922-23, 1929-30 and 1934-36; here he addresses the crowds at the opening of the Guide Hut, with Mrs Barnard, Guide Commissioner, editor Frank 'Spec' Hiddleston taking an assiduous note behind the little boy on the left. Cllr William Moulder, a later Chairman, is looking towards Spec, with George Robinson beside him, and Squire Lowndes rests on his stick on the left with his wife. BELOW: A new King is proclaimed — Edward VIII; the Squire, Vicar, High Sheriff, Chairman and Dr Smith (?) on parade in Broadway.

67

LEFT: In 1937 floods turned the Vale into a watercourse, and Green Lane looked like this. RIGHT: Amy Mill House became a World War II sick bay. BELOW: Goodings smithy in Germain Street, to the left of the then Embassy Cinema, survived the raid, 20 October 1940 — photographed here in the 1950s.

1939-1947 In the second world war, Chesham lost far fewer lives than in the first, but the impact on the town was in other respects much greater. Hundreds of children were at once evacuated from London, and the old St Mary's National School was brought back into use. The Council had already rented the Town Hall from the property company which had bought it; it was adapted as the civil defence headquarters for the town, with P. L. Deland as chief warden and also as Lord Chesham's headquarters for the area. The Council's own office was leased at 33 High Street. The Co-operative premises in the Broadway became a community centre, with the evacuation office, the fuel, food and milk offices, the WVS and the library. The waterworks, which were guarded day and night, provided shower baths and a decontamination centre, and Amy Mill House at what is now Friedrichsdorf Corner became a sick bay. Five public air raid shelters, blast and splinter proof, were erected, but suggestions for tunnelling into the Balks were rejected as impracticable. The churches made their premises available for community use, as did the Girl Guides. Squire Lowndes offered to garage two ambulances at Germains. Miss Alice Warrender of Bayman Manor lent a cottage rent-free throughout the war. A new constitution and rules for the Fire Brigade had just been agreed by the Council; Ralph Howard, its chief officer for many years, thought they could not possibly work, but his successor Fred Paxton proved him wrong.

The Council's peacetime capital programme, always financed by borrowing, came to a halt; there were to be no loan sanctions except of pressing necessity. Elections were postponed, and vacancies filled by co-option. G. O. Bell, elected Chairman in April 1939, proved a strenuous leader in calamitous times, with Andrew Patterson as vice-chairman. He had tried to work closely with the Surveyor (whence the saying that Bell lost his tinkle because he was overgrown with Moss) but by early 1940 their mutual regard was at an end. Frank Moss was capable and decisive, but his private life was open to criticism. The Chairman unwisely convened an unrecorded Council meeting which asked the Surveyor to seek another post. When he ignored this, he was given notice, but the Ministry of Transport declined to accept this dismissal without an inquiry. The Clerk was relieved of the invidious task of presenting the case against a colleague. During the inquiry, which the Surveyor did not attend, the solicitors on both sides agreed a settlement, which he rejected. The staff were in an intolerable position, and Moss was suspended with pay until further notice. Thereupon he sued the Council, the Chairman and then even the Clerk for breach of contract and defamation. The case was not heard until February 1945, when the High Court held that the Council's action was justified but the initial procedure wrong, so that Moss failed against the Council and the Clerk but succeeded in part against the Chairman. There were up to twenty different issues, and costs followed the event on each; finally the Council deemed the net costs irrecoverable. A more serious result was that for five wartime years Chesham had only successive Deputies acting as Surveyor, as well as a part-time Clerk.

As Clerk, Bernard Blaser was inclined to write laconically. Dunkirk was 'the turn events have taken' and flying bombs (a few of which overshot London and hit the high Chilterns) were 'the enemy's present activities'. Geoffrey Bell, on the other hand, denounced 'the ghastly attack made on Chesham' on 20 October 1940, the only one causing casualties. Bombs fell along Germain Street from Gooding's smithy to the school. One recalls that a tottering wall at Weylands was eased back and skilfully re-fastened under the eaves. Another casual attack damaged Milk Hall Farm, and on 17 October 1943 fifteen bombs fell along Latimer Road and cracked the main sewer. Repairs, organised by the Acting Surveyor, W. J. Davis, were swift and effective; little sewage reached the Chess.

The Billeting Officer, H. R. Blundell, had more than a full-time job, and at times the Evacuation Committee was in almost continuous session. The influx rose and fell. In February 1941 Chesham was accommodating a thousand unaccompanied children, 1,848 adults officially evacuated from bombed areas and about 2,500 who had come unofficially. Baths were provided at the rest centre for evacuees, but many local residents used them. Empty properties were requisitioned, unfit houses made habitable, and some condemned cottages re-occupied without permission. The Council completed houses left unfinished in Manor Way, where some frustrated purchasers had already taken possession. New factories sprang up, old ones changed their use, and various workshops were opened, not always with plans and normally without canteens. Chesham had never known such a demand for women's work and hence for communal catering. The Council eventually opened a British Restaurant in the Co-operative Hall, released by the military, and later a second in what had been the Equity Hall and was to become the Council Chamber; these served half a million meals, at the lowest prices in the country.

The war brought some lasting improvements. The Library secured premises at ground level where borrowers had access to the shelves to choose their books, and trebled its issues. The Chesham and Berkhamsted watermains were interconnected in Lye Green Road, allowing the former to supply the latter when it was damaged. The Chesham Fire Brigade became part of the National Fire Service, and secured a new site in Bellingdon Road where the County has just built a new Fire Station.

Vacant allotments were gradually taken up, and temporary allotments secured. At the request of the Bucks War Agricultural Committee, the Council released part of the Nashleigh Recreation Ground for grazing, taking care not to create a tenancy. Permission was given for a pigsty at The Forelands. Waste paper was baled in a shed at the refuse tip. Women were engaged for salvage collection, with 'requisite and suitable clothing'. The Government ruthlessly removed iron railings.

A corporate present for comforts in HMS *Tedworth*, adopted by the town, embarrassed the Admiralty and was returned as the ship's company's gift to the Sea Cadets.

During 1942 the Americans began to arrive, and our civil defenders welcomed them on Saturday evenings at the Town Hall. That winter the Council, confident of victory, began to discuss the town's future. They wanted Chesham to retain its character, part industrial and part residential, but not to grow to a size which would sacrifice its amenities. They welcomed new industries alongside the traditional ones, but considered that this diversification would require expansion beyond that envisaged in 1939. Land had been used extravagantly in the inter-war years, but Chesham had not become just a fragment of suburbia. It remained the shopping, industrial and social centre of a dozen villages, whose life was part of the life of Chesham. If the town was to live, it must grow. Thoughts like these were hardly in line with Professor Abercrombie's Greater London Plan 1944, the basis of regional planning, which would have limited Chesham's population to about 11,500, later eased by the Clement Davies Committee to 13,000. The Council wanted at least 20,000 and eventually secured an 'urban fence' which has had this result. No decision was more important, and none has commanded more consistent support during the last fifty years.

In September 1943 the Council identified preferred sites for its immediate post-war housing development, west of Bellingdon Road and south of Missenden Road. The war lasted longer, but the land was secured and L. C. Powell appointed architect. The Council also staked a claim for 100 prefabricated houses and got 35 for the most needy of all applicants, on redundant allotments and adjoining land in Chessmount.

Fire watching was relaxed in September 1944, and A. C. Sayward undertook the winding down of civil defence. Billeting allowances ceased in June 1945, when most evacuees had returned, though some made Chesham their home. The Borough of Willesden passed a vote of thanks to Chesham. That autumn the Council gave thanks for peace, displayed the Preamble of the United Nations Charter at the Town Hall, relinquished the tenancy thereof, and distributed gifts of food received from the Dominions. The Chairman and F. E.

Howard negotiated the purchase of the Broadway premises from the Co-op in October 1945; the Council moved its High Street office there a year later, and secured the 'old malt house' soon after.

1946-47 was a memorable period for the Council and for Geoffrey Bell, whose service was recognised in the New Year Honours and by his last re-election to the chair. The Council now had its first full-time Clerk, W. I. Nash, a permanent Engineer and Surveyor, W. B. Mitchell, and a new Sanitary Inspector, L. D. Saturley. The housing programme got under way, with exceptionally good work by German prisoners of war, and the Council beat the County Council to secure land in the Cow Meadows off Fullers Hill. A water supply was at last arranged for the Vale, on which four water undertakings impinged. A public convenience was provided for Newtown by the waterworks yard. The warden's post on the Moor became a changing room. As the refuse tips were nearly full, an incinerator was commissioned at Broadwater Bridge. In the Park, the rose arbour over the steps was renewed. The Council's old brown mare had to be put down.

Looking to the future, the Joint Advisory Committee on Planning reviewed Chesham's growth since 1801, joined issue with the Ministry of Town and Country Planning and directed the preparation of a scheme meeting Chesham's demand for development up to a population of 20,000, with protection for open spaces and woodlands, which were thoroughly scheduled. Under the great Education Act of 1944, a Divisional Executive was established for Chesham and Amersham, in which Chesham members played an active part until it was poleaxed by the 1974 reorganisation. The Council lost its direct involvement in higher education, but rejoiced to pass the plans for the long-awaited Technical School at Codmore Cross.

The Council could not claim complete success. They hardly foresaw the growth of traffic problems. An opportunity to buy the Bury and its grounds was not taken; the Silver Prize Band was not permanently revived and the Council could not prevent a large ballast pit below the Moor. Yet this has not drained the Chess, as was feared, and the resulting lagoon may still provide an attractive water feature, of which the Chilterns have too few.

1947-1974 Few towns of Chesham's size were more industrialised, and for Chesham the later forties were years of over-full employment, extreme housing shortage, hope and forward planning. In 1947 only twelve licences for building private houses were issued, against hardship. Of 501 married applicants for Council housing, 462 had no home. The first post-war estate was at

ABOVE: The Fire Brigade moved to Bellingdon Road, seen here in the thirties. BELOW: With peace declared, houses were needed; the Council bought land off Fullers Hill, here in Edwardian times.

ABOVE: Chesham maintained its Baptist tradition — here Zion Chapel schoolroom was all set for Harvest Festival in the 1940s. BELOW: The rose arbour over the steps in the Park — renewed in '47.

Benham Close, and the Council decided that the Housing Manager could well live there. Unoccupied houses were requisitioned; some were not released until 1955. There was a shortage of bricks. The severe winter had damaged roads, yet the Government demanded less maintenance because of the labour demand for essential industries. The Council proceeded actively with other projects. Signposting of footpaths was resumed; houses were numbered or renumbered, and from the ending of Double Summer Time, street lighting was permitted up to half the pre-war standard. A new Town Guide was commissioned. Interim Preservation Orders, which have proved permanent, were made to protect trees and smaller woodlands; the four larger ones had to be left to the Forestry Commission. Consignments of overseas food, and later from Americans at Bovingdon airfield, were distributed to those in need, and slipper baths behind the Council offices in the Broadway were continued until 1964. These offices, rented from the Co-op, had just been purchased, and the Equity Hall became the Council Chamber.

For the first time, the Chairman had a chain and badge of office, presented by the family of F. E. Howard, whose 48 years' service is still a record; his grandfather had served on the Local Board in the 1880s and then on the Council. 'F. E.' was a leader in the religious, social and musical life of the town; a star turn in the male voice choir was his singing of *Queen of Angels*.

The old voluntary library, established in 1923, was professionalised in 1948, though the Council still gave the County Library free premises and, when the Food Office moved to the Labour Exchange, these were extended to include a special section for children. The Women's Voluntary Service asked for a Citizens' Advice Bureau; its establishment was approved on a casting vote.

Among Chesham's greatest treasures is the Park. The Council had leased the Lower Park from the Lowndes family since 1920, but it wanted to secure the Upper Park. On a site visit the resident bull appeared uninterested, and members admired the view from the Rolling Pin. Twenty-eight acres were acquired in 1949 (and one more in 1956), leaving the rest for the County Council, for what became Lowndes School, now Chesham Park Community College. A sixty-year loan was raised for 'public walks and pleasure gardens', but grazing continued for ten years.

For two centuries the special glory of the Park had been its Avenue, but in 1948 this was threatened by Dutch elm disease. A warning was conveyed to Mr Lowndes, then still the owner, but he left the responsibility to the Council, who saw no immediate danger. The County Planning Officer suggested planting a new avenue outside the branch spread of the existing trees. Instead, the Council resolved in February 1950 to fell the Avenue and plant a new one.

No sooner were the trees down (all but three or four were still sound) than some members welcomed their absence. Instead of a full replacement, nine trees were to be planted along the line of the Avenue, with five or six flower beds. The Chamber of Trade and other local bodies asked the Council to think again. The Estates Committee then recommended a new avenue of flowering trees of modest size, but this was lost on the casting vote. In 1958 a petition for an avenue of lime trees attracted 1,400 signatures, again defeated by the casting vote. In 1962 Philip Skottowe asked the Council to plant trees other than elms, more widely spaced than before; this was agreed; the Surveyor was asked to draw up a scheme, but he had other preoccupations. The 'problem' remains.

Chesham had two memorable Festivals. Planning for the 1951 Festival of Britain began two years earlier, including events, a commemorative brochure and 'some undertaking of permanent value'. In Chesham this meant a public hall, and the resulting trust fund kept the idea alive until it was realised 25 years later. Festival gifts of lasting value included the dell on Nashleigh Hill and a fine oak desk for the Clerk.

The Council intended to use surplus wartime and 'Welcome Home' appeal funds to add names to the War Memorial, but it misjudged the Town's wishes by proposing to replace the Soldier by a memorial cross and resite the statue in the Red Lion Street gardens. Instead, the surroundings were improved, though the County planners rejected an ornamental fence as too ornate. The Memorial was rededicated in September 1951. The small island was turfed and has served annually as a garden of remembrance. In the long run, by far the most important decision that year was to acquire for civic development two acres of what was called the Limes site, back to the brick wall in Bellingdon Road.

King George VI died in February 1952 and the High Sheriff proclaimed Elizabeth II in the Broadway with 1,200 children present. That summer the Lowndes family offered the Lower Park to the Town. Appropriately, the name Lowndes Park was adopted, and the conveyance was completed on 30 March 1953, in time for the Coronation. With it there came the seven estate almshouses in Bury Lane, called the Sixpenny Houses from their rents; they were improved, and since 1988 have belonged to the Chiltern Hundreds Housing Association, along with all our Council houses.

Coronation Day was cold and wet, but the traditional bonfire was lit on Dungrove and 230 old people were the Town's guests at a tea and concert. It had been hoped to resume boating on Skottowe's Pond, but the lake was draining away as the water table fell; the ducks and fish had to be removed, and then, a year later, the Pond rose again. At one stage, the Council decided one drake was enough for three ducks and sent the surplus drakes to market.

First steps were taken to provide a crematorium (opened at Washcock Wood, Amersham, in 1966). The Council bought a mechanical road sweeper, and sold the Council's last horse and trappings; appointed a Warden for Townfield, a service so unusual that it was questioned at Audit, and gave active support to a Willesden Self-build Housing Association in Penn and Berkeley Avenues, an enterprise not matched elsewhere in the district. Windsor Road was named after the dynasty, and Patterson and Howard Roads after local families. However, a move to re-revive the Town Band failed, and the Council bought the instruments.

Throughout, the Council's main concern was to meet housing needs. Deansway dates from 1948, and the next scheme comprised Chessbury, Ryecroft and Delmeade Roads south of Missenden Road. In 1949 Aneurin Bevan's new Housing Act encouraged variation in house sizes for different needs. The Council promoted development off Fullers Hill with more than the standard amenities, tenants paying an economic rent. This so alarmed Whitehall that it had to be placed before Mr Bevan personally, and then it had to be staged.

Miss Dawes not only founded a trust which built Dawes Close but also gave the Council a site in Ridgeway Road for fourteen houses. She died before she could sign the conveyance, but her will confirmed the gift. The Council made up this stretch of the road as far as the middle, the other side remaining private and unmade. Next, the Beechcroft Road site was developed with non-traditional houses, not because the Council wanted these but to get houses at all.

In 1952 housing allocations were replaced by targets, but it was not until 1955 that private building accelerated with the Chessmount estate. When refused permission to go further into the countryside, the same developers took over the long projected Hilltop estate, facilitated by a link with Newtown by an improved Cameron Road. The electrification of the railway in 1960 increased incomers, and the available land not already secured by the Council was rapidly taken up by estate developers. The Council had supported legislation to allow the sale of Council houses but, when this discretion was granted, made no use of it. Few tenants or prospective tenants had such aspirations. The population of Chesham doubled and new roads named as follows:

Council initiatives	*Private development*
1954 Chapman's Crescent	Linington Avenue
1955 —	Hawthorn Way, Rose Drive, Kesters Road, Cavendish Road, Eunice Grove, Larks Rise, Shepherds Way

1956	Greenway	—
1957	Great Hivings, Mount Nugent, Captains Close, Marston Close, Durrant Path, Reynolds Walk, Hollybush Road, Long Meadow	The Braid, Cheyne Walk
1958	—	Wykeridge Close, Broadlands Avenue, Barnes Avenue
1959	Cresswell Road, Appletree Walk, Rachels Way, Dawes Close, Chessbury Close	Nalders Road, Taylors Road, West View, Cestreham Crescent, Crabbe Crescent, Brushwood Road, Hillcroft Road, Ashfield Road, Woodcroft Road, Sycamore Dene, Aylward Gardens, Pulpit Close, Harding Road, Prior Close, Pullfields, Garson Grove, Gray's Walk, Hivings Park
1960	—	Nutkins Way, Longfield Road, Crossway, Tweenways, Little Spring
1961	Darvell Drive, Poles Hill Fair Leas	Warrender Road, Lycrome Lane, Freeman Court, Lee Farm Close
1962	Nugent Court, Wallington Road, Elm Tree Hill	Preston Hill, Birch Way, Cherry Tree Walk, Russell Court, Swan Close, Cross Meadow
1963	Deansway House	—
1964	Hill Farm Road, Cannon Mill Avenue, Black Horse Avenue	White Hill Close, Webb Close, The Warren (named by Amersham RDC)
1965	—	Valley View, Portobello Close, Broadview Road, Wesley Hill, Treachers Close, Field Close, Little Hivings
1966	—	—
1967	Hodds Wood Road, Batchelors Way, East Street, The Backs, St Mary's Way	Meadow Close, Copse Way, Woodcote Lawns, Mill Close

1968	Pheasant Rise, Woodland View, Whichcote Gardens	Meades Lane
1969	—	—
1970	Five Acres	—
1971	—	—
1972	Dellfield	Masefield Close
1973	Shelley Road	Partridge Close, Hillside, Wannions Close, Bevan Hill

Beside the flood of new residents from Greater London, there was another influx from overseas to meet the needs of Chesham's industries. A Community Relations Council was established. A growing, more youthful and more varied population made unprecedented demands: schools had to be built; there had been no new first or middle schools for a generation. Heritage House School with the adult training centre and adjoining children's home were provided on surplus allotment land. Deansway House linked housing with welfare in a way which Princess Marina came to admire. The new Library, opened in 1971, was a regional centre on land made available by the Council. The Temperance Hall was bought by the Council and leased to the newly formed Old People's Welfare Committee; the proceeds helped to build the Hivings Park Free Church to serve the north end of Chesham, which finally secured the 'bus service without which some of its older residents would have been housebound.

From 1949 to 1974 the Housing Manager, L. D. Saturley, was also Public Health Inspector; as such he waged a vigorous campaign against unfit housing. Some of his reports make chilling reading, but inevitably they brought him into conflict with the defenders of the Old Town and Waterside, who believed that a wonderful opportunity for preserving and enhancing the character of old Chesham was being missed. Listing historic cottages was no safeguard against neglect and decay, though only one listed building actually collapsed and, if an old house survived the sixties, it was likely to be highly valued and restored. A scheme for clearing the whole of George Street and Alexander Street, the oldest part of Newtown, was realised only in part; many of these mid-Victorian cottages, though lacking amenities, were not unfit and have been improved. By 1970 no slum clearance was in operation, and none was needed.

Although the Limes site had been bought with an assembly hall in mind, a health centre had a stronger claim. In February 1959 Clifford Culpin was commissioned to design Council offices in Lowndes Park, in the vicinity of the farm buildings. He presented a scheme for a hall as well as offices, intended to enhance the Park, leaving storage and depôt facilities on the Limes site. One consequence was the relocation of the paddling pool presented by the Round Table (Rotary gave a scented garden for the blind). Another result was the demolition of the farm buildings, which were built on granite sleepers made for Stephenson's London and Birmingham Railway; some of these are still there. Opposition to any building in Lowndes Park was initially voiced by the Townswomen's Guild; it became vocal at a public meeting called by the Chesham Liberal Association. The Council was accused of a breach of faith with donor W. F. Lowndes, but there was evidence that, unknown to his family, he had himself envisaged a new Town Hall in the centre of the Park. The decision on the Council's planning application rested with the County Council, who received five representations in favour, 4,200 against (4,000 being duplicated letters) and therefore asked the Minister to call it in and decide it himself. Meanwhile the Government imposed an embargo on new municipal buildings, though this applied to offices, not to a public hall. The 1960 election split the Ratepayers' Association and left the Council equally divided. A motion to expedite a Ministerial inquiry was declared 'not carried', but this left the issue open to be raised again and again, and the Chairman, who had tried to sever his connection with all bodies having electoral significance, was finally driven to use his casting vote to withdraw the application. It was never revived and, since the dedication of Lowndes Park to the public in 1972, against the advice of the officers, building in the Park has been precluded.

This debate, however exciting, was peripheral to the main issue before the Council — alternative proposals for the town centre. The inquiry into the Town Map made it clear that the County Surveyor wanted to widen the High Street, while the County Planning Officer supported the Council's long-standing advocacy of an inner relief road. Happily for Chesham the Inspector was Mr C. D. Buchanan, now known to the world as Professor Sir Colin Buchanan, author of *Traffic In Towns*. His report has never been published, but it clearly came down in favour of the relief road. However, instead of including it in the Town Map he deleted it and said that further consideration should be given to its alignment, particularly its junction with the High Street. The proposal, which the Ministry supported in principle, might then take the form of a small comprehensive development area. This neatly shifted the main responsibility at County Hall from the County Surveyor to the County Architect and Chief Planning Officer, Fred Pooley, who was taking a close personal interest in Chesham (he designed the Deansway House complex). His proposal, adopted by the Council on 25 July 1962, sought to get traffic out of the High Street with the minimum of turnings and demolition. It took the relief road from the entrance of Germain Street, across Church Street almost at right angles and northwards along the line of Skottowe's Pond. At the north end of the lake its line bent westwards to the top of Blucher Street, returning by another gentle curve into Broad Street, just north of the existing entrance to White Hill. This was to take all through traffic, local and long distance, leaving the High Street free for shoppers and for service. The scheme left as much as possible of the Limes site inside the relief road, in order to house as many public buildings and facilities as possible. Commercial development on the High Street frontage was envisaged to help to pay for civic development on the backland; this is the one feature of the plan not yet realised.

The County Surveyor was unconvinced and uncommitted, but that very morning the Ministries of Transport and of Housing and Local Government issued a joint bulletin on the redevelopment of central areas affected by traffic congestion. A plan for the centre as a whole was indispensable. This represented the spirit in which planners and Councillors rescued the centre of Chesham from intolerable congestion. Implementation was long delayed, and even now the ultimate aim of a pedestrian precinct has not been completely achieved, since not all trade premises have rear access.

An immediate issue was what to do with the old Town Hall, which had been bought by the County Council for highway widening, after 25 years of neglect. The Chesham Society, formed to defend Chesham's distinctive character, wished to reactivate it for meetings, plays and concerts. The Townswomen's Guild agreed, but the Chamber of Trade, while supporting the relief road, made the singular suggestion that Skottowe's Pond should be filled in as a site for a new hall, municipal buildings and car parking. In April 1959 the Ministry had promoted the Town Hall from the supplementary to the statutory list of historic buildings, but the County Council wanted to demolish the clock turret as a dangerous structure. The Ministry asked for deferment, temporary repairs and a conference, but by then the County Council thought the whole building should be demolished. In Chesham Council a motion to this effect was declared 'not carried' but the Council asked for first refusal of the clock. A report commissioned by the Chesham Society proposed that the 1856 extension be removed and the original small Market House restored. The Society could have financed this, and the Council was inclined to meet its maintenance, but meanwhile everyone waited for the town centre plan. *A Future for Chesham* was a splendid document, but it was long delayed, and the delay proved fatal. By January 1964 the Town Hall, with its turret and tiles gone, was such a wreck that the Council asked the County Council to demolish it, but to agree to the construction of a clock tower as a focus for the High Street and a feature at the town entrance, incorporating the original turret clock and whatever else was worth saving of the materials of the old Market House. The County disposed of the Town Hall and Chesham acquired the whole Market Square, its use defined as 'an amenity area including a clock tower or some other similar feature'. That took nearly thirty years.

The Town Map regulated the outskirts as well as the centre, but this was less contentious. The Chiltern countryside is so beautiful and so vulnerable that it needs and deserves all the protection the law can give. The draft Map, first proposed in 1952, sought to set limits to the built-up area, but to increase the Town's open spaces to about 150 acres. The Green Belt was defined and, except to the north-east of Chesham, most of it became an Area of High Landscape Value; this in turn served to define the Area of Outstanding Natural Beauty, formally designated by the Government in 1965, the highest category short of a National Park. This is managed by the Chilterns Standing Conference (since October 1994 the Chilterns Conference).

The Council acquired Lye Green, Big Round Green and other manorial wastes in 1957, though not the lordship of the manor. Negotiations were started for Captain's Wood, which was eventually bought by the County Council and approved for formal designation as a Local Nature Reserve. The Council bought Marston Field in 1958, the Co-op Field in 1959 and Codmore Field in 1963; but Chesham is short of level land for sports grounds to relieve pressure on the Moor.

The Council has tried to ensure that rights of way are legally defined and properly maintained. In 1950 there were believed to be 101 footpaths and bridleways within the town boundary; there are at least 120. Hearings on the definitive map in 1954 resolved some disputes, especially round Dungrove, where the Council's first lady Chairman testified that she had used one track since the relief of Mafeking. One path created by agreement runs beside White Hill on the top of the bank.

In 1961 the Earl Marshal granted the Council a coat of arms, including the swan and buck, the chessboard, two beech trees against a cornfield, red and gold mantling and the motto 'Serve one another'. The Chairman who secured the grant presented a new jewel, the old one being re-engraved for use by the Vice-Chairman. The Town Council has inherited the arms and regalia.

In 1964 the Surveyor's office was destroyed by fire; the County Council made the Three Tuns (then on White Hill) available, but most drawings and records were lost. Riverside Court replaced the old centre of the hamlet of Waterside. The reconstruction of the overloaded sewage works was started. Chesham and Amersham became a Parliamentary constituency. Above all, the goodwill of the road engineers was secured, and the first stage of the relief road, gratefully named St Mary's Way, was opened on 15 July 1968.

The idea of a Chesham (or Chiltern) Festival of the Arts surfaced in 1965, and a Council Committee was soon established, its first project an orchestral concert. By 1967 several organisations were involved, and the 'Festival of Chesham' was promoted by a Town's Committee with sports, youth, arts, theatre, church and social interests. Amersham was well ahead with provision for indoor sports, including swimming, and in the long run Chesham could look for dual leisure provision at the High School, but the immediate demand was for a theatre which could also be used for films, banquets, dances, mannequin parades and so on.

In October 1968 the Mozart Players came to Cestreham School and the Festival Committee set June 1970 as its target date, to celebrate a thousand years of the Town's recorded history. The programme was agreed by February 1969. The Council offered the Chamber for an exhibition by two local artists, Val Biro and John Young, and allowed the Festival Committee to use the civic arms, displayed on a town flag presented by the Chesham Society. The Council gave a guarantee against loss. The Festival lasted from 24 May to 7 June, with a remarkable range of activities: drama, light opera, a fashion show, a 'Chesham 1000' exhibition, Gillette Cup cricket, tug-of-war, recitals, ethnic music and dancing, and inaugural, youth and civic services. The Chairman of the Council attended all these, once by helicopter; recalled to the chair in the Millenary year, he sought to establish the Lady Elgiva as a significant figure in national as well as local history, and the Chess Valley Archaeological and Historical Society gave the Council a copy and translation of her will.

The Festival year saw the Drill Hall become a youth centre and, with the Sea Cadets moving to its annexe, the old malt house of Chesham Brewery was refurbished to provide a Council Chamber, committee room and a modest public hall. The Conservation Area, the first in Bucks, was extended and defined. The splendid mural over the chancel arch of St Mary's, depicting the events of Holy Week, was dedicated. Main drainage was extended to Botley, Ley Hill and Lye Green.

There was one failure — the town's doctors indicated that, without full agreement on a health centre, for which the Council had promised a site, each practice would go its own way. This removed the last but one obstacle to the Elgiva Hall. The Council now had the site, the ideas and the intention, but not the money. Even this last difficulty was soon unexpectedly removed.

For many years the Rickmansworth and Uxbridge Valley Water Company had coveted the Council's water undertaking, alleged to be too small to be efficient. The Company's first offer in 1955 was rejected as derisory. Members felt that water was an asset which should belong to the community, but already nationalisation or regionalisation was in prospect. In 1959 the Government reactivated the 1945 Water Act and promoted regrouping. A more attractive offer from the Company was reluctantly accepted by 9 votes to 8, in view of the Minister's indication that he was prepared to use his statutory powers to enforce a merger. The agreement was sealed, but proved abortive at the last moment. Objections were made and then withdrawn, but the Company allowed the time limit for Ministerial confirmation to run out without seeking an extension. One suspects that, in view of rising interest rates, they regretted their 'first and final offer'. By the end of 1971 it was clear that water companies would continue, but that on reorganisation, local authorities' undertakings would pass to regional water authorities without compensation. The Company made a new offer, less favourable than before, but with a promise to maintain differential water rates in Chesham for five years. The Council accepted in November 1972 and, with capital funds in prospect, at once consulted local theatre groups (of which this book's editor was a spokesman) on the design of a theatre-hall. A brief was rapidly agreed and entrusted to Clifford Culpin and Partners. This time the Order authorising the sale of the waterworks was unopposed, and it was approved just in time for the transfer on 1 April 1973. There was a twelvemonth to start the civic hall, for which Chesham had so long yearned, before the Urban District Council finished. To keep costs within the available funds, external works were set aside and the fly tower reduced. The only tender, just within the limit, was accepted on 8 January 1974, subject to planning permission; this was received from the County Council on the 19th, with the praiseworthy but expensive conditions that the roof should be of natural slates, not asbestos cement slates, and that there should be a landscaping scheme; the hall was not to rise from a sea of cars. A transfer from the allotments account found the extra funds and, at the Council's last meeting, there was extreme pleasure, mutual congratulation and grateful thanks. Earlier that day George Malin, designated Treasurer of the new Chiltern District Council, had handed to Ken Marks, Town Clerk of the incoming Town Council, a cheque for £180,000.

The glory of the Park — the Avenue — felled and not forgotten, but not replaced either; from a 1930s postard.

The Urban District of Chesham ended in a flurry of activity. The Malt House was completed and inaugurated with an exhibition. John Kay House, named after the late Surveyor who designed it, was opened. With Cromwell House, on the site of Cromwell Terrace, it formed a fitting climax to the Council's work for the housing of old people, begun in Townfield and Fullers Close. This had been the special concern of Tom Scott and Kath Harries, the last Chairman, who chose all the furnishings. Her last act was to unveil the magnificent Chesham Tapestry, the gift of the Chesham Arts Society. A presentation copy of the booklet describing it is the last entry in the Urban District Council's last minute book, but the Council's last action was the Civic Service on 31 March in the Church of St Mary, Patron of Great Chesham, whose lilies are in the civic crown. The Council gave thanks for eighty years of service and handed on to the Town and District Councils its hopes for projects not yet achieved.

ABOVE: In 1960 the Chesham railway line was electrified. Here the old steam shuttle pauses at Chalfont Road that year. (LTE) BELOW: Much excitement was generated about the town centre, relief roads and High Street traffic. Meanwhile the Town Hall was a bit the worse for wear, with no clock tower and no slates.

86

ABOVE: Once down, the traffic flowed a bit better, but the Market Square stayed 'empty' for thirty years. Much more has changed since St Mary's Stage I opened 15 July 1968 and East Street was constructed, in this early 1970s view. BELOW: Footpaths matter, and the Council watched over rights of way; one path runs beside White Hill — not much more than a footpath itself in this early 20th century postcard.

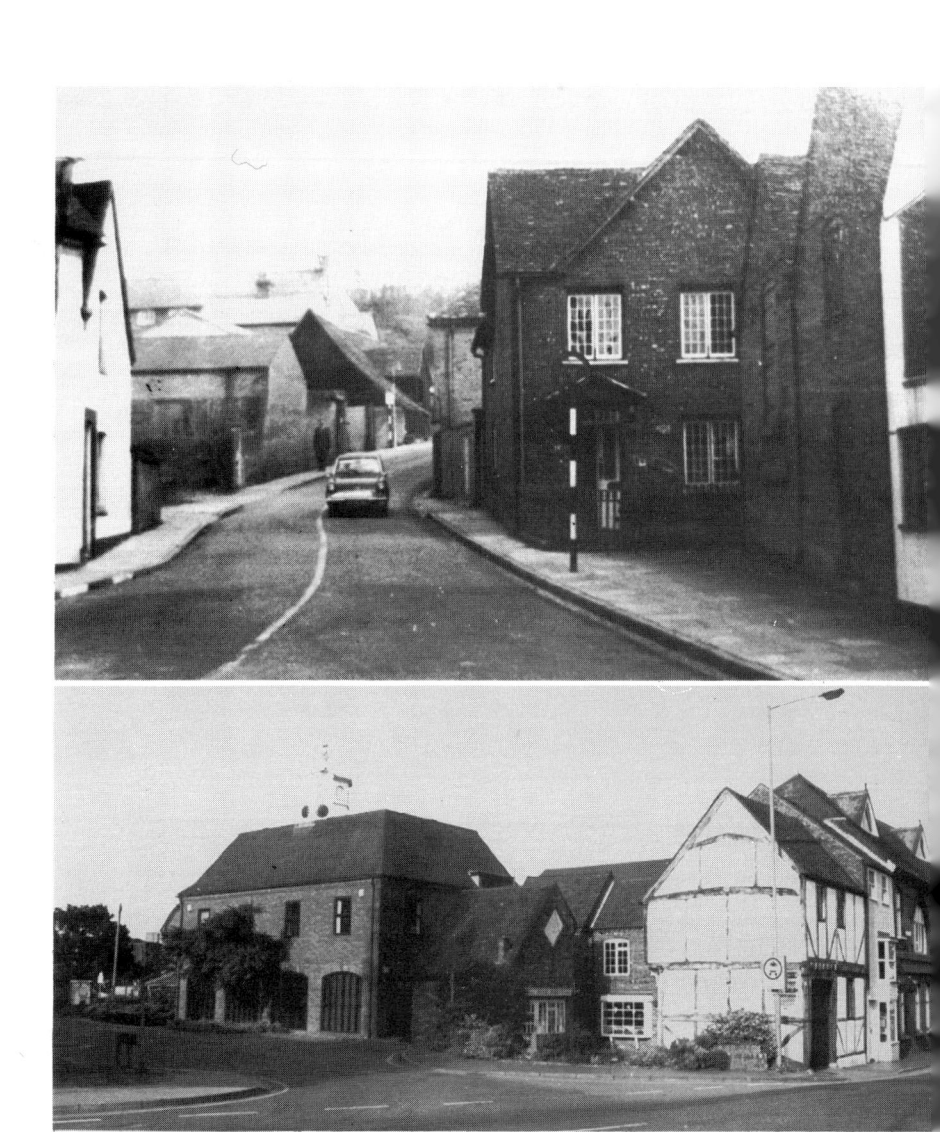

ABOVE: White Hill had improved by the time the Surveyor moved to the Three Tuns — its site explains the bend on the hill where the open space sits; the Plough inn is on the left in this 1950s picture, the brewery sheds and stables beyond it; the brewery offices were in the gabled building facing the camera. BELOW: The Malt House was ready for Council use, as the old Urban District bowed out. The timbered structure on the right was once the butchers' shambles, and later Chesham's independent vintner, Climpson's; Equity Hall, the building on the far right, housed the Council chamber and offices.

1974-1994 The inaugural meeting of the Chesham Parish Council took place on 12 October 1973 and, for a short time, Chesham was served by two masters as Councillors switched their allegiance between the Urban District Council and its successor authority. With the Urban District Council's assets and responsibilities set to transfer on 1 April 1974 to the Chiltern District Council, the incoming Parish Council fought to retain its most treasured possessions.

The assumption of Town Council status from 1 April was passed unanimously and a Steering Committee established to negotiate with Chiltern the transfer of property and services which Chesham believed should be managed at local level. Top of its shopping list was unquestionably Lowndes Park.

In what has now become known as the Malt House Treaty of 24 January 1974, agreement was reached for the retention and ownership of the Town Council of all parks, recreation grounds and open spaces (including Lowndes Park and the Moor); statutory allotments; the Malt House and the Temperance Hall; the War Memorial; 'bus shelters and street seats; land for the proposed building of Elgiva Hall and the theatre itself, when erected.

The future of Chesham Cemetery, previously administered by the Chesham and Chartridge Joint Burial Committee, was soon resolved. Chartridge Parish Council relinquished its interest and responsibility transferred to Chesham Town Council from 1 April. Residents of Chartridge still have a right of burial in Chesham Cemetery but at double fees!

Not everything went the Town Council's way. It lost control of the town centre car parks to the District Council and gave up street lighting to the County Council after just one year.

In 1975 the Town Council embarked upon an ambitious project involving the construction of a footpath alongside the River Chess from Lower Moor to Cannon Mill. The Riverside Walk, now part of the Chess Valley Walk, was completed in July 1976 at a cost of £3,500. The former watercress beds at Red Lion Street were reclaimed in 1979, for the Meades Water Gardens on land given by J. R. and Miss C. J. Garrett-Pegge, which received a certificate of commendation from the Civic Trust. In 1983 the Council inaugurated a Family Tree Scheme in Lowndes Park. Organised by the Tree Council, this is one of only seven in the country and allows individuals to fund trees to commemorate family events or in memoriam. A Parish Tree Warden was appointed in 1992.

With the money from the sale of the Waterworks safely in the bank and with interest accruing, an Elgiva Hall Committee was established. The upper cost limit was £185,000. The Hall opened its doors for the first time on 26 February 1976 but trouble was just around the corner. Within twelve months, Douglas McMinn offered to purchase the Hall for £150,000, plus a donaton of £50,000 towards running costs in Trust, and to turn the Hall into a day centre for pensioners, blind and disabled as a registered charity, letting the Hall in the evenings. Although the offer was rejected by the Town Council, the proposed buy-out provoked immense public interest. Constant disagreement in Committee about future policy invariably led to a bad press as the Town Council employed a succession of hall managers and staff, until finally in 1984 Alan Jenkins & Associates were appointed agents to manage the Hall. This marriage lasted six years until the District Council became the Town Council's new partners on 1 April 1990, an arrangement which continues.

The sale of part of the Council's Taylor's Farm allotment site to Harman the builders in 1985 for close on half a million pounds triggered negotiations with the District Council to secure a leisure centre. The Town Council had been considering this option in 1975/76 when a scheme for the development of Chesham Moor was submitted by Longstone Investments. This project was not promoted because resources were already tied up in Elgiva Hall, but it was resurrected ten years later when the Town Council pledged a £200,000 interest-free loan to the Chiltern District Council.

The opening of the Leisure Centre in 1988, the Town Council's capital loan having been secured the previous year, allowed the District Council to end its lease of the swimming pool on the Moor. The following year, the Town Council took back the asset which now provides open air swimming throughout the summer under the management of the Chess Valley Sports & Leisure Association Limited, a non-profit making community management company established by the District Council and supported by Chesham Town Council.

The County Council produced plans in 1989 for the pedestrianisation of Chesham High Street. A Clock Tower, on virtually the exact location of the clock of the old Market Hall, was promoted by the District Council and received considerable support. Particular attention was paid to detail so that features from the old Town Hall could be reproduced while ensuring the structure was in keeping. Constructed in local brick, manufactured and donated by H. G. Matthews, brickmakers of Bellingdon, the Clock Tower includes the original dial, hands and clock mechanism lovingly restored by Smith of Derby. The only concession to technology is a small electric motor to wind the mechanism. The Town Council earmarked £66,000 towards environmental features within the pedestrianised High Street and applied £58,000 for the

Pedestrianisation has calmed traffic in the High Street.

construction of the Clock Tower. Mrs A. F. Hooker, a former Town Mayor of Chesham, gave a generous donation towards the cost of restoring the original clock faces, in memory of her husband.

Since the end of the Second War new international relationships, contacts and friendships have developed between towns here and elsewhere in Europe. A public meeting on 19 March 1980 discussed formal twinning between Chesham and Friedrichsdorf and received resounding support. The formalities soon followed. In 1986 the partnership was extended to Ville de Houilles in France and a third twinning partnership with Archena in Spain is planned for 1995.

The improvement of town amenities and environment are Town Council matters; in the past five years, Chesham has acquired new and safer play equipment; a new sports pavilion at Codmore Field; major improvements at Elgiva Theatre and the open air swimming pool; hanging baskets and ornamental flower beds; town centre Christmas lights; the establishment of an environmental forum and Chesham Youth Council, and a safer town with the installation of closed-circuit television surveillance cameras.

ABOVE: The Elgiva Hall — Chesham UDC's financial swansong after eighty years of good housekeeping, and the Town Council's achievement, asset and liability. BELOW: The Clock Tower echoes the old Town Hall.

ABOVE: Industry along the Vale has acquired a pleasant face. BELOW: Townsend Road School is no more, but forms the basis of contemporary housing.

ABOVE: Chesham Council fought for continuity. It won the battle; by contrast, the town has lost in other ways — Lord's Mill, the symbol of local industry, on the site of Elgiva's achievement, is no more. BELOW: Other losses include Amy Mill, after a lorry hit it, somewhat fortuitously hastening its demolition.

WISE COUNSELS

The 1974 reorganisation of Local Government was contained in the Local Government Bill published in 1971. There was no provision for any form of Town Council or Parish Council in those areas of existing urban district and boroughs to be absorbed in the new and larger District Councils. Existing Parish Councils in rural district areas were to remain, for example, Amersham Parish Council.

At the Annual Conference of the Urban District Councils Association held in June 1971, a Chesham delegate spoke to a paper entitled *A Town Needs a Town Council*. It highlighted a serious omission in the Bill to provide any form of successor Parish status. Following the Conference presentation, the Chesham Urban District Council decided to launch a countrywide campaign for the creation of successor Parish Councils in towns with a population below 40,000. The case was argued at length in a document which, together with a copy of *A Town Needs a Town Council*, was sent to 569 Local Authorities. Considered replies were received from 116 of whom 85 saw a need for a Parish Council (or some equivalent body) as their immediate successor in their area on 1 April 1974.

At the same time letters were addressed to the Department of the Environment, the Urban District Councils Association, the Association of Municipal Corporations and Timothy Raison, Member of Parliament for this Division, seeking to persuade them to this Council's views but without, unfortunately, any success. In a letter dated 15 July, the Secretary of the Urban District Councils Association stated 'The [Reorganisation of Local Government] Committee adhered to the previous decision to accept the Government's proposals on the grounds that such interim Parish Councils would be a divisive force in the new Districts but they would tend to prejudge the review by the District Councils and that if the Government got the new Districts right, the special interest of existing Districts would be adequately safeguarded pending the review'.

On 27 September 1971, a letter came from Timothy Raison, MP enclosing a copy of a letter from the Minister which stated 'I recognise that there is considerable concern in the smaller Boroughs and Urban Districts, but there will be no authorities to succeed than specifically in those areas from the 1 April 1974 when the new system of government comes into operation'. A consultation paper explained that there were two reasons; the most important was that the establishment of Parish Councils in such areas from 1 April 1974 would mean retaining the separate identity of many towns in a way which would be bound to detract from the unity of the new District concerned. The other reason was a practical one; the serious problems in electing and setting up such Councils between the District Elections in the Autumn 1973 and the appointed day, 1 April 1974.

'In our judgement it will be best to allow the new District Councils to become firmly established before decisions are taken on the setting up of Parish Councils in small towns. But I am, of course, considering carefully representations made on this part of the Government's proposals, along with the other representations made on this consultation paper, and I can assure you that I shall take the Council's views into account in reaching my decisions.'

The Urban District of Chesham was to amalgamate with the Rural District of Amersham. It was difficult to see why the creation of a Chesham Parish Council should detract from the unity of the new District whereas a continuance of the existing Amersham Parish Council should not. The population difference between the two areas was less than 5,000.

The Chesham campaign was not without its lighter moments. In an article seeking national support written by the Clerk of the Chesham Urban District Council and published in a Local Government journal, he concluded as follows: 'Finally, may I make reference to the Chesham and Chartridge Joint Burial Committee, if for no other reason than to highlight an absurdity which the present proposals will create. At the present time this Committee administers the only cemetery in Chesham. The constituent members of the Committee comprise this Council and the Chartridge Parish Council. The Local Government Bill specifically preserves the interest of Chartridge (population 1,750) in this cemetery but, at the same time, equally specifically removes the direct interest of the town of Chesham (population 21,140). The irony of the situation is that Chartridge Parish Council will probably be delighted to divest itself of this particular service'.

Time moved on and the Royal Assent was near. It was beginning to look as though the campaign had failed when a telephone call was received from the Department indicating that the Minister had decided on a last minute amendment to the Bill. Provision was to be made by the insertion of a fifth part of Schedule 1, providing for the constitution of Parishes by reference to existing Urban District and Borough boundaries. Creation of each Parish would require an Order by the Secretary of State and suddenly alarm bells were ringing yet again. It was rumoured that approval would only be forthcoming for the creation of Parishes with a population of less than 10,000 people; Chesham's population was 21,140. Fortunately, it was only rumour. Application was submitted, the Order was made

Many local shops have gone, but some remain; Garlick's has moved.

and Chesham Town Council existed. Although, compared with the Urban District Council, the powers of the Town Council were somewhat truncated, nevertheless, there would be some government of Chesham by members elected by the townsfolk. As one optimist was heard to say: 'Who knows? The new Council may carry on to the millennium in 1994' — but that, at the time, seemed a long way away. It has now happened and the town's motto 'Serve One Another' remains as appropriate today as at any time in the past 100 years.

ABOVE: An asset — the pedestrianised High Street. BELOW: High Street was well shopped in the fifties too.

SERVE ONE ANOTHER

In this world you can be sure about two things according to an ancient proverb, and that's death and taxes. Chesham Town Council is, of course, involved in both of those. It controls the cemetery where the team will be glad to bury you. It also takes a little of your hard earned cash to provide a wide range of local services and facilities.

During the compilation of this chapter I had occasion to descend into the bowels of the Town Council Offices. There I found Clive Birch and our Town Clerk, Mike Kennedy, burrowing through mountains of old minute books. They were researching our past. I looked around the room containing the last hundred years of minute books. I noticed that they all had one thing in common — they were all bound. The colours differed, the condition of the books differed, the size was approximately the same, the dates and the contents differed but they were all bound. That's about where the similarities finished. I delved into these books going back to the 1890s and I saw a lot of handwriting. The structured writing of the old Town Clerks had a certain precision and beauty as they laboriously minuted what had taken place. As the years passed there were changes. The handwriting changed, not necessarily for the better, sometimes it was legible and sometimes it was less legible. Out of the blue, I came across some typewritten minutes. Then I discovered some which had been duplicated on a spirit duplicator. As I passed through the years there were some that had been duplicated on what I would call the old Gestetner duplicator. That's the one where the typist has to 'cut' a stencil using a heavy-duty manual typewriter. Then, as I moved further on, I found minutes that had been typed and then photocopied. Finally I found today's technology, the minutes created on a personal computer, then printed on a laser printer. So from this, I suppose, we can conclude there is one other thing that you can be certain of in this life and that's change.

The publisher of this book seems to think that, as Town Mayor, I am the keeper of the 'official' crystal ball! So I will look into the glass and try to guess, gauge or imagine what the future may have in store. Gazing into any crystal ball is, of course, a difficult and thankless task. Some things are clear, some things are less clear and some things are just obscure. Before we go on this flight of fantasy I would like to show you where I think we are today, and what Chesham's strengths are. There are weaknesses and opportunities but above all let us also recognise the threats.

One of the greatest strengths of Chesham Town Council is derived from its birthright. It was born from the remnants of the old Chesham Urban District Council. Chesham UDC was well known and respected by the local community. Everybody in the town knew their Council and where it could be found. The Town Council that we have today grew from that background. Parliament looks upon Town and Parish Councils as being the same type of local government. This does both types of Council a disservice. Chesham Town Council has always had a large breadth of services and facilities to manage, with a budget to match. On the other hand, some of the ancient Parish Councils do not want or even feel able to handle such responsibility. Towns and parishes might have been grouped together by statute, but in real terms they deliver different services.

In Chesham there is an office staffed by loyal and dedicated professionals who can call upon a grounds maintenance team with a 'can do' attitude. The workforce is always led by an experienced Local Government Officer. Our current Town Clerk is no exception being qualified with a Certificate of Higher Education in Local Policy (Local Council Administration). The Councillors, who come from the community, meet regularly as a Council, and it is their local knowledge that gives strength to this, the lowest level of Government.

Councillors are committed to seeking what is best for Chesham. As a Council they make representations to other levels of Government, Statutory Bodies and Quangos about issues that affect the town. Together they act to ensure that recreational and leisure facilities are available for all the people of Chesham. Assets include Lowndes Park, Elgiva Theatre, The Moor, Marston Field, the open air pool and many more. The Town Council is even subsidising the Chiltern District Council's leisure centre at Chesham High School, because, without that money, it is probable that no facility would have been built.

However, there are weaknesses in the system. The government does not fully recognise the real potential of Town and Parish Councils. This is evident in the current Local Government Review where the Government has refused to force unitary authorities to devolve functions to the lowest level possible. Perhaps this was the result of strong Town Councils being locked together with Parishes that just have no desire to play in a bigger field and provide more services to their communities.

Over the coming years there will be many opportunities for the Town and its Council to contribute towards an improved Chesham. The pedestrianised High Street is an asset. It has a beautiful Clock Tower, provided and maintained by the Town Council. There are safe walkways and it has easy access from a major car park. However, its full potential will not be realised until all the shops have some form of rear, or controlled, access. This would enable more imaginative uses to be made of the streets — perhaps more entertainment, perhaps pavement cafés and displays; the possibilities are endless. There are currently a number of empty shops. This too, in its own way, is an opportunity. Is it time for rents to come down? There is a serious economic crisis that may be slowly drawing to an end. With the current level of interest rates everybody, including landlords, will have to accept a lower return on their investment, and that must mean lower rents.

The UBM Pratt site, opposite Waitrose in the High Street, is a large development opportunity within the town centre. It is probably the largest one that we are likely to see for many years. The opportunity should be taken to encourage a large store into the town. People keep mentioning companies like Marks & Spencer, Woolworth, etc, but any of the larger chain stores would draw people to the town. The opportunity should also be taken at that time to improve the Town Council Offices. This could be done by perhaps including the existing offices and the Malt House in the same development package. This would enable the offices to be improved both for the staff but especially for the public. The opportunity could also be taken to improve access for the disabled.

One of the highlights of 1993 was the formation of the Chesham Youth Council. Consisting of councillors drawn from all the local schools it provides a focal point for the 10% of the town's population who are of secondary school age. During their first term of office many new ideas were generated. In the future they will have the opportunity of making a radical contribution to the services and facilities that are offered to the youth of Chesham. Meanwhile, on the Town Council there are no Councillors under the age of 40, although there will be the opportunity to change that during the elections in May 1995!

A major threat to the shopping centre and to the vitality of Chesham is the development of out of town shopping complexes. Large supermarkets built away from Chesham, that people can only get to by car, threaten our small and traditional traders. This issue will have to be confronted. These supermarkets and out of town trading centres, in the end, cannot be beaten; they can be restricted but not stopped. Another threat to our very way of life is what can be loosely termed petty vandalism and minor crime. Chesham is not a high crime area but, like other towns, there is some mindless vandalism, damage to flower beds and seats, smashed bottles, glass in the paddling pool, etc. Finally, the other threat to Chesham over the years has taken many forms. They took away the magistrates' court, the main police station and they even tried to take away the fire station. So what is left for them to take away, to centralise? One has to ask, how safe are our libraries? How safe, if you like, is the Town Council? Will the government's next move to emasculate local government be to remove Town and Parish Councils? This is what I call creeping centralisation, and that is a big threat.

As I sit in this hot and humid summer of 1994 the government is carrying out a radical review of Local Government. Some would say that, having lost overall control of all bar one of the County Councils the Government is now intent on destroying them forever. My own view is that, although it would make 'good copy', that explanation does not stand up to scrutiny. What I find more plausible is that, given the trend to privatisation, centralisation and tighter government control of the purse strings, indepth local democracy and accountability is no longer thought to be essential. As far as the general public is concerned the whole business has really been one big yawn. They are being asked to express a preference, not in a referendum, but by returning a paper to indicate whether or not they prefer one of a number of different options. There is no guarantee that anyone will take any notice of their vote. Whatever is implemented it is certain that the number of Councillors, the number of people representing or serving the people of Chesham, will reduce. Obviously, if this can make Local Government more responsive to the local people then it should be applauded. From Chesham Town Council's point of view, it may be a wonderful opportunity to take on more responsibility to deliver local services by what is the lowest, most local level of government.

If we look to our twin towns in Germany, in France and our prospective twin town in Spain, with a similar population level, they enjoy a greater control of their services at a local level than we do. The Town Councils of Friedrichsdorf, Houilles and Archena have many, many more powers than Chesham and services are delivered at the most local level possible. As I look into my crystal ball I would like to think that Chesham will have similar advantages in the years to come.

As I look into the future, there are some things that are clear. It is certain that closed circuit television (CCTV) is coming. As I write work has already started and, within a short while, we will be switching on the first CCTV system, probably in the country, for a small town like Chesham. Why did we do it? Obviously it is a method of combating petty crime and mindless vandalism but that is not the only reason. We believe that Chesham is the best town centre in the area and that we have to give the traders every advantage and opportunity that we can. Closed circuit television enables our car parks and our town centre to be safer.

Safety is important. But for our Town Centre just increased security is not enough. During the coming years we will see it change. We have to accept the realities of shops like Tesco for they service a need, people are using them and, in their own way, they are successful. However, we must ensure that out of town shopping precincts do not kill off our town centre. I have a vision of a town centre where people walk freely; where they have the opportunity to browse; the opportunity to pause here and there; to window-shop; to drink coffee, beer, wine or orange juice. It will not be easy running a shop in the high street of the future. In some segments of the market competition from 'tele-sales' and 'out of town centres' will be fierce. The days of popping into the local shop to buy a pint of milk or a can of beans are, I am afraid, rapidly disappearing. Everybody should be supporting the local friendly milkman by having milk delivered to the door! But the beans will probably be bought in one of the larger supermarkets. Traders will need to identify a niche market that is uniquely theirs to be successful. It will be part of the Council's job to encourage and enable people to spend more time in the town. This will only be possible in an environment where parking is less restrictive, cheaper if not free. Traders must also be allowed to put out tables and chairs and display their goods outside their premises. The Town Council will need to work together with traders to attract more people into the town centre.

Chesham has a history of which it can be proud. The provision of a Town Museum and better sign posting will give everyone better access to our heritage. Tourists could be attracted by active marketing in the hotels and guest houses of the capital and surrounding towns. When the CrossRail project is completed Chesham will be within easy reach of London. This must be viewed as an opportunity, not just of reducing the commuting time of city workers, but also of attracting visitors to our town.

Further into the future the effect of 'the information super highway' will be seen. As business markets become saturated computer manufacturers will turn towards the home user, who may well ask 'Why do I need a computer?' The answer will be found in the facilities available and the cost of telephone lines. How often have you wanted to buy a theatre ticket or a match ticket and been confused by all the different descriptions and prices. Where is seat H20 at the Elgiva? A computer system is already being tested in America that will answer such questions by putting you 'in the seat' and showing you a real video of the view. Next, imagine that you

The UBM-Pratt heartland site is an opportunity.

want to book the Malt House for a wedding reception — how do you want the chairs and tables set out? With the systems of tomorrow you will be able to design the layout in your own home and be sure that is what you will get on the day. Better still, for those of us who do not like reinventing the wheel, why not look back at other peoples' layouts! If you want to report a problem then perhaps the computer already has the answer. If it does not then ask again the next day to find out when it will be resolved. Who is buried where in the Cemetery? Where would you like to be buried? How much of my Council Tax is being spent on flowers? Which flowers? Where are they planted? All this information could be on the information super highway. The salespeople will not be selling computers or software, they will be showing their customers how to get onto the highway and access information.

Will Chesham Town Council still be here in another hundred years? Who knows? It is certain people will still die and need to be buried. It is also certain that the inhabitants will be taxed. I suspect that the Town Council will just be one of the service stations on the information super highway. It will be easily recognisable though, because your computer screen will turn claret and blue and the following words will appear — Serve One Another.

The CrossRail project will bring visitors, and speed the workforce back and forth, rather faster than yesterday's old steam shuttle.

ABOVE: 'They' took away the Police Station — here to let. BELOW: Chesham's setting in the Chilterns remains the same — symbolised by Cholesbury Common in the winter of 1937, looking towards the town. (SHF)

A Town for Today

There are so many truisms about Chesham, so many truths. A Cheshamite is someone born here — incomers are welcomed, but acceptance comes with the second generation. That is part of the town's duality — warm but wary, prosperous but puritan, helpful but sometimes harsh. On the road to nowhere, and a town which was forced to export its hardwon product 1,000 years ago, Chesham has forged a steely independence from its ironspring past. That is why it led the fight for local power in 1974, why it retains its own paper and why it has the world's oldest building society. Most important, it is why so many come to stay, stay to serve, and if they leave, remember it well and with abiding affection.

In 1954 there were two building societies, the paper was under threat from competition, predators and uncomfy owners, and the trains were old, slow and dirty into our cul-de-sac terminus. Woodwares dominated, but plastic was upcoming, the Council was justly proud of its good housekeeping, but pressed to permit tall buildings, new homes private and public, and roadways bearing little thought for future need or past presents, like the core Town Hall, Georgian butcher or Amy (Amen) Mill. The industrial heritage epitomised by Lord's Mill was endangered, the Football Club was slipping, Gilbert & Sullivan was filling the Embassy Cinema and Labour balanced Ratepayer in a quietly Liberal electorate. Then as now, you could stand in Broadway and see green hills, north, south, east and west.

To a professional observer, there were two towns. One was the cash town, known for its 'beer, boots and brushes', and its craftsmen like saddler Wilf Cox, puckish on his stool, stitching and binding boot, bag or briefcase, expansive Giff Newton, supremo of boot manufacture, the Barnes boys with their woodwares and the Wrights with their sawmills and timberyards. There were men in aprons behind counters, like Reg of Derrick's, steak surgeon and quip cracker, oddjob builder Dave Talbot, who took the old Market Hall to pieces, neat Dicky Rose, whose chef's hat and trim moustache presided over many a public banquet, foot-gowned Tilly Stillman, who kept her hair up, her lodgers in their place, and a grand salon with Kitty Hearn's antique wares, so you never knew what chair or table next to expect.

There was dancing Dixie Dean, sometime woodware maker, with his gliding wife Helen, and his white Rolls Royce, Griff Griffiths of the Embassy Cinema, who patrolled the aisles and hooked out hooligans before they could lob a single sweetpaper onto the stalls, and there was laughing Ray Ulyett, who kept Lizzie's Bonce — the best pub in town down Church Street, nurturing youngsters and serving old timers alike, always a Sunday lunch for the lonely hearts touched by his sweet wife Phyl.

There were ancient names like Puddephatt, Darvell and Plested, proud stores like Brandon's, pubs like the Blue Ball, Tap and Crown, stern schools like Lowndes under Grosstephan, and fair justice with coppers like Coulson and McIlroy backed by a Bench under Clapp and Garrett-Pegge. Here were the bad boys whom we all knew and quite liked for their predictably limited violence to property and respect for their fellows. Here were the myriad churches and as many pubs — churches and chapels, for two Baptists had shared a wall, and there were three more; pubs had saloon and public bars, but in the Queen's Head these were interchangeable.

There were aliens assimilated like German Laurie Kress, interned, released, naturalised and king of the Atlas pencils, who liked a gamble, and electric genius Ted Stuart (née Tchaikowsky) whose hand magicked life out of redundant tellies and hi-fi sets, and who knew about the gulag, behind German lines and MI5.

And there was the other town, with extroverts like Reuben Shackman, jeweller to the rich and famous, and the only people who could weave gold thread; Doug McMinn, pedlar turned millionaire-loner, whose staff worshipped his autocracy, fairness and success — and shared it right to the end, when he made many of their fortunes; Andy Melville, who gave Winston Churchill his annual Christmas turkey, and was the nearest to a squire we had, at Lowndes' Bury; Kitty Hearn, great Guider and antiquerian (sic); Stan Cox of the saddlery family, who headmastered and sang the old songs; Leo Chittenden, who retailed hi-fi and lit the football field; Bryn Morris, who mended mouths and Tom Wise who thought it was all in the mind and was invariably medically right; Val Biro, Hungarian incomer-artist, who presided over parties at Germains and drew record sleeves, until Gumdrop made his way; Nye Bevan, who wandered, poetry in hand, across the Broadway, the least verminous gentleman farmer in the land; Frank Hiddleston, who ran the paper for 50 years, wrote most of it for 26, sported weskit, wing collar and cherubic cheeks, penned *The Trivial Round, the Common Task*, and was known as Spec; Charlie Yorke, music critic and proofreader, who made the past word-perfect; Tessa Reynolds, one of three sisters with the Primrose Cafe — High Street cakes and tea, bettered only by the Ainley Taylors' morning coffee midst antique tables at the later House of (Kath) Tree; Billy Nash, who sold the brewery, bought a pub and spawned an Olympic bobsleigh champ; the list is endless.

There were men of substance like Cyril Howard, of cherubic mien and public service, John Ellis, perenially concerned with property, players and propriety and Andrew Patterson, who chaired Chesham's paper and its clothing emporium and died as he served, in public — at a council dinner.

There was a natural succession of family business, with Askews, Larkins and Catlings — men of probity who founded Table, grew their firms and helped the handicapped. High Street nameboards were like memorials and seem immortal — Murky Pearce, ironmonger, whose Aladdin's cave held everything possible, and a good many less likely; if he couldn't help you, Goodings would, at their Germain Street forge. There was old man Gutteridge and his two sons, tall men who fitted allcomers with hired, bespoke or off the peg suitings with grave faces and courteous banter. There were the effervescent Treibers, Nettie coiffed and encased, and Solly fussing about the latest couture, Chesham-style. And archetypically Chesham, with the sibilant ess, was genial Jim Climpson, a man not to ruffle, who taught a generation vinous delights, bearing tots of nectar in his backroom basement, and carrying half the town and all the pensioners on wine or stout tick.

Chesham was a classless town. It had its rich men, its Pond Park people and a sprinkling of nobility in and around, but in those days of separate saloon and public bars, the town ran without rancour, its priorities not social division, meaningless to dustmen or bobbies on the beat, church or chapelgoers or people in trade, but outsiders and all their works. The enemy was not within, but without — in Amersham, London Transport or County Hall. And the town took pride in its urban district status and specific performance. Certainly, we often complained about service or costs, but year in, year out, we returned a balanced chamber, with Ratepayers Baines and Brandon, Socialists Scollay and Moulder and Independent Commander Fred Jackson, of the Royal Bucks Laundry, who kept clean witness for us all.

And the town sang — in choir, music hall and true D'Oyly Carte idiom. It played as well — six-a-side cricket, Carnival, serious football in the lower leagues. It raised money and spent it wisely — on almshouses, cottage hospital and pioneering property like the Fullers Hill development of higher income public housing. It helped the helpless, through Rotary and Round Table and countless other charitable endeavours. It put on a good show, with theatre club and Broadway carols.

Framed in memory's lens are cars parked in High Street, kids congregating on the Electricity corner, queues for the Saturday morning children's cinema, coffee at Ainley Taylor; conflicts outside the Co-op Hall with coppers clipping earholes of a Saturday eve, Christmas carols in the Broadway and orderly crocodiles converging on Skottowe's park for cubbing, scouts or guides; raucous fairs ranged down the Moor and fun and games for after-school kids up the Rec near the Nash; ancient blue Rover 'buses collecting kids and the brewery dray trundling thunderously down Broad Street; timber stacked high between Germain and Church Streets, cows in Catling's farmyard at the foot of Park Road; a bottle of pop and a bag of barleysugars from the Duck Alley sweetshop, a second hand cycle from Mayo and Hawkes and late night groceries from Chesdale Stores; dusty documents at Botley House on John Francis's backroom shelves, Tudor ghosts among the cobwebs in the cruciform attic of derelict Lord's Mill and the last of the cressbeds near the old railway inn down Bois Moor Road.

In 1954 the town was small, independent, prosperous, friendly and isolated. The commuters had not yet come to town — they found Amersham more accessible, cosmopolitan and tolerant. Hilltop estate, electric rail, the not-far-off M1 motorway, all conspired to change the self-sufficient, introspective not to say insular, town into what it is today. Forty years later, Chesham has the obligatory pedestrian precinct, the chain stores, the empty shops. the car parks, dual carriageway, fast food, splendid schools, public buildings and urban sprawl of any other town 29 miles from Marble Arch. It has fewer churches and far fewer pubs, better trains, a clocktower but no town hall; it has lost its natural nexus 'twixt Church and High Street and thus its historic shape, but it has kept its most important treasure — the personality of the place; it changes people, they do not change Chesham. Long may it remain thus.

It becomes easier to understand when you read the records — for a start, the 16th century parish registers abound in Birches! That's a long past. Ben Boughton has lived within some four miles of Chesham most of his life. His outsider's inside view defines the place. Sarah and John Dodd ran Chenies Mill, leased from the Duke of Bedford. Sarah's nephew (and Ben Boughton's grandfather) took over in 1857 at 16. In 1871 he leased Manor Farm. Agricultural depression in the 1880s meant the rent was short. 'To everyone's surprise the Duke forgave him two years rent'. The Dukes were not universally popular . . . hard landlords . . . one of the functions of the village was . . . to act as a dumping ground for discarded Bedford mistresses and offspring, who arrived married to an estate worker suitably recompensed. Grandfather made his family promise they would never allow a bad word about the Duke or his family . . . an injunction passed onto me when I was four years old.'

Ben Boughton's father took over from 1915 to 1933; Ben was born in 1927 and the family leased land from Lord Chesham at

Latimer as well. When that was reclaimed, 'Dad did not exactly eulogise the said Lord and my early memories were confused by the relative merits of the unimpeachable Duke, the rather doubtful Lord and the good Lord who sent the rain and sun — it took a long time to unravel the complexities and functions of aristocracy and the Deity'.

Part of the business was supplying animal feed locally and the young Ben Boughton went on his rounds with George Tomlin by horse and cart three days a week, to Chalfont Road (today's Little Chalfont) and Chalfont St Giles, to Chorleywood, Loudwater and Sarratt, and to Chesham and Latimer. These incurred visits to Cox the saddler for harness repairs. 'Wilfred was the person George saw while the grandfather was a wizened old man with a bowler hat tilted up at the front, perched on a stool busily stitching but saying nothing.' The late Joe Darvell, 'gave me a receipt from my grandfather for flour delivered to Chesham in 1908 . . . in those days there were no car parks . . . cars parked in the street or six places surrounding the war memorial in Broadway'.

There was a 'regular order for a bullock to Clays the butcher in the High Street, near the new Post Office. The unfortunate animal was unloaded early in the morning before the town got busy and goaded down a narrow passageway to the back of the shop where it was slaughtered in conditions . . . not quite up to EEC standards. The business was managed by a Mr Loveday, who had a terrible limp; the floor was covered in sawdust and in a raised corner sat Mrs Clarke, the owner's daughter, who handled all the money'.

Then there was Harry Wing, tenant of the Golden Ball with a 'prosperous business in collecting dead and casualty animals from farms and transforming them into dog and cat meat in the outbuildings . . . adjoining the pub. Local farmers and ancillary business [people] gathered there to do business . . . Among the regulars was Harry Hearn, a bowler-hatted gentleman who owned three cattle lorries along Bois Moor Road, driven by Wilkins, Sherman and Frank Wallington'. The Hearns are still in transport. Johnny Cope was a cattle dealer whose lorry was driven by Ernie Hawkes, brother to the Red Lion Street cycle retailer.

'Harry Wing was . . . completely untrained in veterinary matters . . . but a better diagnostician than any vet, a skill he passed on to his son Harry, who still farms at Broadway Farm at the top of Hivings Hill . . . Collecting dead animals, farmers [the Wings] called on were often in a state of stress and Harry being a kindly man . . . became their confidant. Uncle Tom, founder of T. T. Boughton, was very religious and . . . did not frequent the Golden Ball much . . . but on occasion unloaded his troubles on Harry. In the mid-1930s he was let down by a customer for around £10,000 and it was touch and go; he went to Harry for advice . . . Harry said nothing but went out of the bar and returned a few minutes later with four biscuit times: "Here you are Tom, there's two and a half in each of these — let me have them back when you can."' Such was 'the relaxed way in which friends operated in those days . . . safer than banks.' They 'sold one another cattle most weeks and met to square up perhaps once or twice a year. Harry Hearn sent his bill perhaps once a year . . . never a single argument about a bill although the horse trading to establish the price could take hours and a considerable amount of whisky. Harry Wing continued working almost to his death in 1964. The business was . . . unpleasant and the smell . . . pervaded clothing and skin. Harry junior went to the pictures at the Embassy and noticed four empty seats, one on each side, one in front and one behind.'

While at Challoners, Ben Boughton remembered two things about Chesham in the war years: 'During the winter of 1943-44 I was in charge of the footballs'. Shortages meant footballs were unobtainable; the five school balls were not in good order. Every time they were inflated they split, which meant a trip to Cox's. 'Wilfred Cox had a reputation for being a little slow with repairs. "Is 10 days alright?" When you went to collect he would eventually find it untouched and solemnly promise to do it quickly. Footballs were a different matter . . . always ready the next morning.' The charge? 2d or a major repair might be 4d.

Dental treatment was in a room at Germain Street School — 'A lovely white haired old lady was the dentist and the drill was treadle operated, her arm parallel with her leg as she operated it, the pain was excruciating . . . but her strong-armed assistant Miss Grover, who seemed to have innumerable arms, held difficult patients still.'

'Although I have never actually lived in Chesham it will always be my home town,' but the developments in the last decade have been wasted opportunities. 'The Waitrose complex . . . specially designed so customers have to push trolleys uphill across a busy road — why did they not bring White Hill down what is now the top end of the car park, through the coal yard to connect with Station Road, the car park to its west level with the shop? St Mary's Way : with Bellingdon Road traffic down to the northern roundabout and two pedestrian crossings, an unnecessary bottleneck has been created. St Mary's Way is too narrow for four lanes, yet bounded by wide footpaths hardly ever used; from Broadway roundabout to the end of the car park is so constructed one can only walk on it with difficulty. Traffic flow from St Mary's Way to Germain Street is illogical, with precedence over the main road.'

Ben Boughton's views find an echo in those of native Cheshamite George Piggin, who sees other changes, not all for the good: 'The Chesham in which we live today is a vastly different Chesham to that in which I lived as a boy some seventy years ago. Then, the great majority worked in the town itself, or were employed on surrounding farms. Commuters were few. Virtually everything for everyday life was obtainable — almost all from private traders, who greeted you when you entered their shop, served you with courtesy, and often — especially in the case of grocers and drapers — offered you a chair.

'Now we have gone full circle. Our population has grown three times — mainly post-war, when large estates around the outskirts were developed — and the traditional industries, "beer, boots and brushes", have almost died. In their place, we have a great variety, calling for skills of every description. Hundreds commute to London daily, spending two hours travelling. Many also commute to High Wycombe, Slough, Hemel Hempstead and Watford. Virtually all private grocers have disappeared in the wake of the supermarkets, where service is somewhat impersonal. While few private traders remain, Chesham Building Society, Pearce's the ironmongers, Cox's the saddlers and Chapman's the jewellers still give personal service.

'I suppose it was inevitable, but pedestrianisation of the High Street had done nothing for traders. If the Street had been left one way, with restricted parking (*free*) in the wider parts, it would have enabled those passing through to see our shops and realise what we have. On a recent walk through the High Street, I counted a dozen empty shops, plus a couple of large untidy cleared areas which may one day be developed. This does absolutely nothing for the town's image.

'In spite of all that, Chesham still remains a pleasant place in which to live. Our glorious Chiltern countryside can still be reached in very few minutes — long may the Green Belt survive, with its network of public footpaths and our Conservation Area must also be carefully guarded against development.'

Edward Culverhouse was a teacher and a man of property. He bought his first slum house in Duck Alley when he was 22, renovated it, sold it on and bought six more. During the Boer War he built Mafeking and Ladysmith in Bellingdon Road, married in 1900 and moved in. He had three children — Edward John (Eddie), Henry Robert (Bob) and Alice/Alison Rose (Rosie). Now Alison Horsnell, Rose remembers: 'one could walk or cycle anywhere day or night without fear — favourites were Captain's Wood through Billy Catling's meadow into Asheridge Bottom, along the Backs and the Slypes.' Trapps Lane too, where her parents were engaged: 'My father used to say "That's the stile"!'

Culverhouse senior taught for 40 years at White Hill School. A self-taught pianist, he played the organ in local churches and even gave evening classes and private lessons. A councillor, he chaired the Chesham Building Society, was Treasurer of the Property Owners' Association and Secretary of the Ratepayers. He also organised the Hospital Fête at the Bury, which culminated with 'the firework display over the river Chess.'

Mrs Culverhouse was Alice Mary Chance, 'a model of domesticity, wonderful cook and dressmaker. I was dressed daily in petticoats, knickers and dress all handmade with layers of Buckinghamshire lace, goffered and stitched, clean on every day. The teachers sent me round the school with a note: "Look at her underwear." I couldn't understand why they all lifted my dress up!' And every day her rose-growing father sent her to school with a fresh rose for the teacher. Miss Jane Morrison was the Head.

The family moved to the house associated with them for many years — Glenthorne in Bellingdon Road. They died there in the early 1950s, the house was sold, razed to the ground and Albany Court stands on the site today. Brother Eddie emigrated to Australia, married and came back, to raise six children. Eddie Culverhouse was a teacher and served the council too. He died in 1972.

The family tradition extended to brother Bob, who became a teacher and also went to Australia, returned, emigrated to Africa, lost two wives to accident and ill-health and married again, to die shortly after.

Great events marked the Culverhouse saga, like the flood of 1918 'when Chesham streets were waist-deep in water. My father was playing the organ at Chesham Bois Church and my mother sat in the bedroom window watching the water rise and wondering how my father would get back home — he left his cycle and walked home down the Backs.'

Not long after the move to Glenthorne, 'there was a big fire at Webb Jarratt's factory, late at night ... I watched it from my bedroom window ... what a spectacle!' Then there was 'the great freeze in 1918 when the pipes froze and burst and White Hill School had to close for a month. We had a wonderful time, skating on Skottowe's Pond and at Shardeloes and tobogganing on Dungrove and Second Park.'

Happy memories of childhood, 'riding round Chesham in my goat-cart, attended by my brothers; my father bought me a little two wheeled cycle, a rarity in those days, and I cycled everywhere,' and memories of a different way of life: 'we were brought up to work, given our allotted chores . . . the boys to tidy up the orchard, feed the poultry, pick the fruit and I to clean the silver, the knives, and polish the furniture. We also had a lot of homework, the leading article of the *Daily Mail* for dictation every day and to say the French for everything at the dinner table.' Those were indeed the good old days.

At about the same time in the 1920s Ron Hodgkins recalls Chalk Hill — 'just a cart track cut out of the hillside. If you climbed the steep bank to the left at the summit, green fields stretched for some distance, many wild flowers thrived . . . on the other side . . . allotment holders toiled to grow vegetables to supplement their meagre incomes. My late father had a plot next to William Moulder, who served the town faithfully for many years.

'At the foot of the Hill stood Mr Keen's dairy. He served milk straight into customers' jugs from his back door. If you turned right towards Hivings Hill, especially during school holidays, you had to take care to avoid the four wheelers which regularly whizzed by . . . constructed with old pram wheels and wooden boxes.

'Farmland extended right up to the junction with Asheridge Bottom . . . a short distance away you came across Payne's Farm; one building by the road provided children with an ideal goal . . . looking left were the old stone cottages known locally as the Pest Houses, near the present entrance to Deansway, demolished in 1938 for a new block; most of the residents were rehoused in Pond Park, then being developed. Deansway was formerly an old cart track, an ideal playground; the only thing to watch out for was Woodley's horse and cart — he owned a field at the top of the lane where the local social club played cricket.'

Then 'the end of the 1939-45 war saw a massive change; the beautiful trees and bushes were felled to make way for Deansway, Benham Close and the surrounding area. Another magical playground was lost forever.'

In post-war years myths abounded, some founded in fact, some less so. It was said that Chesham had the highest illegitimacy rate in the nation, that our delinquents were more numerous than elsewhere. The reality was more prosaic. There were local rowdies but more visiting thugs, a little light larceny but thieving incomers, an occasional real crime but most of the major action was up the Hill, and this is borne out by the town's most famous lawman. Retired Detective Superintendent Malcolm Fewtrell was born in 1909 and came to Chesham in 1933; 'a young and naive policeman, I found lodgings with a Mr and Mrs Ben Grove in Gladstone Road. Typical of the natives . . . an honest and charming couple. For my room, full board, washing and ironing I paid £1 10s a week.' After a year the young bobby joined CID.

'So far as Chesham was concerned there was certainly no need for a CID man but the . . . Eastern Division under Supt John Neal covered . . . Gerrards Cross, Penn and Amersham and these stockbroker belts were a housebreaker's paradise. We were successful in detecting . . . for one very good reason . . . no matter how much money, how many fast cars and sophisticated equipment the police will never be successful . . . unless they have the wholehearted support of the public. We had that support in those good old days . . . time after time we would find . . . a neighbour had noticed something . . . sometimes contacting us when the offenders were still about.'

Young Fewtrell married in 1934 and stayed in Chesham until 1938, when he went to Aylesbury. 'Happy memories of Chesham. Dare I say it, a somewhat sleepy town, which some of the older residents had never left, even for a day. They were all so friendly and helpful. Dr Catherall, before the days of the NHS, was tireless and never sent a bill unless the patient could afford to pay.'

And the shops: 'my wife . . . spent something like ten shillings a week at Kingham's in Broad Street. They supplied a little notebook for her order; this was taken to the shop and the goods were delivered the next day. The following week another order was written in the book and last week's paid for. The local milkman was Ernie How, who drove round with his horse and cart, came to the door, filled one's jug with the regulation pint measure plus a little bit extra "for luck".'

One close friend was Stan Cox, saddler Wilf's brother and headmaster of Whitehill School — 'he enjoyed intepreting the local dialect. One day I was a bit puzzled when I heard one boy tell another he was "frit toller" until Stan explained he was "afraid to shout".' Industries were wooden wares — 'shovels, spades, butchers' trays, bowls, hoops and so on, leather goods, brooms and brushes, so called Clarke's field boots which, though packed and sent out in Clarke's boxes, went nowhere near Street, and of course the watercress beds in Waterside . . . serving Covent Garden.

'I remember a likeable and extraordinarily astute young man called Douglas McMinn who was certainly not one of Stan Cox's most brilliant pupils, who started his own business buying seconds from local factories and hawking them round the town, eventually building a multi-million pound wholesale empire.

'The squire of Chesham then was Mr Lowndes and prominent were the Garrett-Pegges, both magistrates who presided at what was then called the Police Court next to the Police Station . . . another amiable magistrate was Fred Jackson, a retired RN Commander who ran the local laundry. Local estate agent Cyril Howard was a pillar of the establishment, his brother Phil the Town Crier. All I remember him crying was a regular "The water will be turned off from . . . to . . .". Then there was editor Hiddleston, a most friendly, genial and hard working man, not averse to hitching a lift in a police car.'

There was the day when the *Examiner* was 'caught' by a so-called letter to the editor (yes, this editor and publisher!) following an article about Roman remains. 'The letter was published in full on the front page, claimed the writer [now believed to have been John Broad] had a piece of broken pottery bearing the inscription "Iti sapi spotand iti sabi gone." There were a lot of red faces in the editorial room.' (Confirmed — the chief reporter had a fit, I had a laugh, the general manager nearly had a coronary and we were forced to apologise in print but we had the last laugh, because we sold out; even the *Times* asked for a copy!)

Mr Fewtrell returned to Chesham in 1950 as a Detective Inspector. 'Things hadn't altered much, Chesham itself almost free of serious crime although I did have a murder in Townsend Road one Sunday lunchtime. Still plenty of housebreaking in the rest of the Division,' but there were CID at Amersham, Beaconsfield and Gerrards Cross. 'Five happy years followed — with people like Eddie Greenham (builder), Camille Heistercamp (Shillakers, bag manufacturers).' And thence to Aylesbury, still responsible for Chesham 'a very law abiding place, unlike other parts of Buckinghamshire.'

It is 30 years since Malcolm Fewtrell was here but he keeps local contact and takes the paper. 'It is obvious the town has changed a lot and not for the better. Sadly the old 1931 police station has gone . . . supermarkets replace the small friendly shops and as for serious crime, the place seems to get more than its fair share. Sixty years on I still have happy memories of the town and the friendly people who welcomed a newcomer.' And thus to fame: 'I was about to retire in 1963 but you may recall there was a little bit of trouble on the railway line near Cheddington which delayed my departure.' A modest man and a friend of Chesham, Malcolm Fewtrell was the man who caught the Great Train Robbers.

In the thirties the Melvilles arrived. Daughter Nancy Haslehurst recalls 'My parents were looking for a bigger farm. They arrived in Chesham by taking a wrong turning in Tring. The Vale was flooded — weird in high summer. In the High Street was a shop, Maison Melville. Dad said "Our relatives are here already!" Another turn and we were in Pednor Road. A noticeboard showing "For Sale" advertised the Bury Farm. My mother said "Stop the car. I've come home". That was in 1937.

'The farm was derelict, but we loved it: the undulating countryside, beechwood, the peace of Chesham, lying snug in the palm of a hand whose fingers stretched towards Amersham, Rickmansworth, Hemel Hempstead, Berkhamsted, Great Missenden.

'The Second World War brought amazing changes to the sleepy town: the flooding (by soldiers this time), with a Divisional Headquarters at the Bury, and Latimer as part of MI5. Bombed out firms re-located in Chesham. Van Houtens from Holland made chocolate and George Williams produced army clothing, both in barns at the farm.

'Melville Turkeys was the first firm to produce turkey portions and pies and sell them in our shop. The St John Medical Comforts Depot in Chesham was the first of its kind and I helped to set this up.

'Chesham is a super little town and I am always glad to come home.'

A later owner of Bury Farm is Anthony Moss, Sheriff of the City of London in 1992-1993: 'based at the Old Bailey, I much looked forward to returning to Chesham . . . when duties allowed . . . I wish it was possible to spend my working life here.'

Born in Star Yard (now the car park) in 1917, Robert Gomm was sitting with his wife in Chesham Park one day when the church bells started *Days and Moments*. 'What is that tune' she asked, and he explained it was played at noon and midnight. One thing led to another, so he set down his boyhood memories:

'I started at school at 3½ years at Germain Street Juniors. We used to sleep in cots in the afternoon before going home. We had a rocking horse to play with. Then I went to White Hill, run by a Mr Dodd, a very strict Headmaster. I knew the feel of the cane like my left and right boots (it was boots then, not shoes). Later on his job was taken over by Mr Stanley Cox. If you were ever late, Stan would give you two of the best on each hand, but he was quite a fair man for sometimes he would call you to his study and present you with a pair of trousers or socks that he had cajoled out of a local trader. In those days we were always hungry. As the school overlooked the Chesham Brewery, if the wind was in the right direction we could smell the beer too.'

From school to play time: 'We used to go birdsnesting along the ivy-covered walls by the church and up by Squire Lowndes' walls that ran up to what was then known as Second Park, a big field above the park, and to the then lovely ring of elms.

'We went camping too in Second Park. The tent consisted of old sacks; our food consisted of birds' eggs, usually moorhens' or perhaps a few ducks' eggs taken from the Squire's lake, and a few potatoes raided from the Pednor Road allotments. We built tents in trees called barries, short for barricades.

'In those days the Park pond was just a reed-lined mud pond, with a small island, well rat-infested. We used to make rafts on the pond but usually finished up in the mud, which meant a good hiding when you got home. Later on they built a proper edge and had boats, for which the park keeper charged four people one shilling an hour. When your hour was up the park keeper would call you. We used to pretend not to hear and rowed away around the other side of the island.

'On one side of the lake was a lovely row of walnut trees, real big ones. We used to bash the walnuts down; if the park keeper appeared on the horizon the cry would go up: "Parkie". We used to run like the dickens because if he caught you he had the full permission of your parents to box your ears.'

Robert Gomm remembered the market too: 'It used to stretch from the market cobbles right down to Germain Street. There was a man who sold bananas and we must have looked a bit hungry, for he would throw a few to us. I remember there used to be a huge negro all in chains and locks trying to escape, and a man selling his own brew, which was supposed to cure anything from warts to old age.'

To between-wars children there was free entertainment:

'In those days there were three highlights of the year — the Summer Carnival, the Fire Brigade procession and the Hospital Fête held in Squire Lowndes' grounds. At the Summer Carnival Mr Catling, whose business it was to collect local factory goods to take to London, had a son who dressed up as a cowboy and local men on his carts dressed as Indians. George Ottaway dressed as John Bull, and another character as Felix the Cat. We never knew who he was but we used to pull his tail and he would thump us if we couldn't run fast enough. At the Fire Brigade Carnival 16 Fire Brigades from all over the area turned out. It was a torchlight procession with the Church Lads Brigade, an RAF band from Halton, Boy Scouts, Girl Guides and all of the Youth Clubs. The Hospital Fête gave a marvellous firework display at the end of the day.'

There were also pranks and problems:

'Life was hard but tranquil, and it seemed that every other man was a poacher. If caught poaching he came up before the Beak, and would be fined ten shillings, a lot of money then.

'Ironmonger Wallace in the High Street had one entire window devoted to guns, ferreting purses and rabbit snares, but most people made their own, and Brown's in the Broadway also displayed these wares. He sold carbide power for cycle lamps; with water it made a gas and gave a wonderful light. We used to get hold of it to make explosives — put some in a bottle, add water, cork it quick, toss it and it exploded.

'The town had a large number of sawmills and most of the wood was carted. These carts had a long adjustable pole and if the trees were long enough we sat on the poles for a ride, but there was always someone who would shout to the drive "Whip, whip behind", he would leap off his seat and whip around the legs as we scrambled off.'

Then, children made their own fun:

'In the Broadway, there was a horse trough with a tap at one end where people on bicycles filled their carbide lamps. We played marbles in the Broadway. When you had a ring of marbles you had to scramble them out if you saw a car or a vehicle coming, then try to place them back in the same position but there was a lot of cheating.

'In the winter when there was snow, White Hill provided the best illegal bobsleigh ride in Chesham. We used to make our own sledges then — two pieces of somebody's fencing nailed together with slats across the top.' Robert Gomm died in 1993.

With war came evacuees. Not all of them were London children. Past Chairman of Chesham UDC and Town councillor Kath Harries remembers:

'After being bombed in Northolt without warning one lunchtime in 1940, we came to live in Chesham. At first, we lodged with a kind family, but in 1941 we moved to a house in Chartridge Lane. I went to Northolt with a removal van to get our furniture.

'When we arrived back, it was raining. The van could not be unloaded so we had neither curtains for the windows nor beds to sleep in. My mother and I slept on the floor. We put our baby daughter in her cot in a cupboard.'

With those memories once more emerges the recurrent theme of Chesham's generous welcome to newcomers:

'As soon as the furniture had been unloaded, we went shopping. On our return we found food on our doorstep. I asked my neighbour which shop had delivered them, but to my surprise she told me they had been left by local people who were sorry for us. A note had been put through the letter-box saying, "My husband will come at five o'clock to put your curtains up". That was the only person I could personally thank.'

Kath Harries ends by saying 'I publicly thank whoever you were for the kindness and friendliness I have so many times received from the people of Chesham. I am so happy here and would not want to live anywhere else'.

She is not alone, for Hermione, Countess Ranfurly adds her recollections: 'About 50 years ago my husband and I drove into Chesham for the first time. We'd bought a house nearby and needed to go shopping. In those days you could drive up or down the High Street and park for a while outside the shops. Somehow I managed to leave my purse, ration books and licences in one of them. Returning home I found them all awaiting me — they'd been returned by the shop owner even though he was busy and we lived miles away.'

Lady Ranfurly comments that 'Though the town has had to alter to suit present day traffic . . . nothing has changed the people. They are the best in Britain for friendship, help and loyalty and no-one can challenge them,' and she ends with this unreserved praise: 'I would record my gratitude, admiration and affection for the citizens of Chesham — unswervingly — for over half a century.'

The forties brought others to Chesham, none more closely involved with its post-war past than Town Clerk W. Ivo Nash. He writes: 'I started work in Chesham at the beginning of 1946 as the first whole-time Clerk, and I found the Council vitalised and ready for Town development. Among the first jobs with which I was concerned was finalising the costs of a High Court Action in which the Council had been involved, and clearing up the costings of prisoner-of-war labour which had been working on the services for the Bellingdon Road and Missenden Road Housing Schemes. The Billeting Officer was still here, and clearing up, and we completed agreement between the Council and the Showmen's Guild for transfer of the Fairs from the Broadway to the Nashleigh Recreation Ground.

'We were soon to receive the report and advice from Professor Abercrombie upon development in this part of the Chilterns — in particular the very limited extent to which Chesham should develop.'

Mr Nash continues: 'The Council was responsible for the public health and ancillary services, highways maintenance and improvement of carriageways and footpaths, water supply, car parks, house building and maintenance and letting, etc, the levy and collection of rates and rents, land charges, byelaws, town planning, loans for house purchase and grants for home improvements, the making and amendment of assessments for rating valuation, and so on.

'The administration throughout had to extend to cope with the expansion of the services provided by the Council, and this I think the Council did very well. Councillors were enthusiastic and knowledgeable, and they had officers and staff who worked well as a team — to do the best possible for a rapidly growing town.' Then he focuses on one of the Town's most contentious issues:

'The greatest problem that has confronted Chesham over the years has been that of traffic through the High Street: greater traffic choked the High Street, and the solution chosen was that of a dual-carriageway Relief Road, favoured by the Urban District Council even though the County Council thought the problem should be tackled by widening the High Street.

'The proposals for a dual-carriageway, prepared in the Chesham Offices, went off to the Ministry of Housing and Local Government. Well, H.M. Treasury pressed for approval of a single-carriageway only, as a first stage. That is what actually happened, and we had one-way traffic in the High Street and in St Mary's Way.

'I left the Clerkship in 1969 and years later the second stage of the Relief Road was implemented with two-way traffic in St Mary's Way, and the High Street a very attractive shopping precinct.'

He ends with this compliment, 'Apart from the pleasure of walking and shopping in the High Street I would like to say what a delightful feature is the Town Clock! It shows what can be done to provide amenities as well as necessities, when the will and the means, exist!'

Those times of Ivo Nash's recall centred on the fifties when, as another incomer observes: 'Chesham sprang into the second half of the century ... the wartime spirit glimpsed in the D-Day commemorations pervaded every sphere of local activity.' Peter Larkin's father Fred had moved into Springfield Road with his wife and three sons in 1947.

'Making a greater contribution than they thought then, Chesham councillors ... were vociferous in a call for manufacturing ... without detriment to local amenities ... to ensure economic stability. There was a mushrooming of amateur dramatic, choral and orchestral societies and community associations ... new housing areas ... at Chessmount Rise, at Hilltop and at Great Hivings and industrial centres at Springfield Road ... Asheridge Road ... and existing factory sites.'

There was 'growth in print, light and medium engineering, specialist domestic and garden products, storage and distribution' reflecting older companies like H. Hearn; many like Cave Wood expanded further afield. The Larkins started the first factory in Springfield Road, appropriately enough Larkin Forge Ltd, laminated spring manufacturers. Chesham has always achieved a certain symmetry, for Mineral Lane remembers long-ago spa waters not far from Wallington's lemonade factory; Skottowe's Pond mirrors lost liquidity; New Road says it all where Amersham's concerned; Amen Lane is the end of the town and Higham Mead reflects low-level waters; the spectre of the Three Tuns still obstructs downhill traffic at White Hill and Eskdale Avenue is one of the steeper hills. And then there's Eunice Grove — well-named for location as well as family ties.

In 1950 the Larkins 'noticed a timber-hauling cartshed and shire horse stable within a hundred yards of their home . . . in disuse.' They moved their business from Edgware. 'The roof of the cartshed had collapsed and was jacked back and secured.' When the shed was replaced 'its component parts were carried out through the new building's doors, new built over old without loss of production.' Then the replacement was damaged by fire, broadcast on the BBC news — '80% of the staff appeared by 9' on a Saturday morning 'worked through day and night to ensure production by 7 am on Monday' which the BBC confirmed; 'this spirit of loyalty and enthusiasm . . . renowned in pre-war and wartime Chesham remains in 1994'. Larkin's original 1800 square feet became 18,000; merged with the Woodhead Group in 1973; replaced by Larkin Distribution Services, now part of H. Hearn & Son, in its fourth Chesham generation.

Peter Larkin remembers the parallel growth of engineering firms like Shackman of Waterside, manufacturing jewellers, precision engineers Carsberg of Asheridge Road, boilermakers Frederick Kay and aircraft equipment fabricators, Flight Equipment & Engineering and Flying Service Engineering, Blease Medical Equipment, Hivac, Sundt, Van Houten, A. F. Grover, L'Oreal, SPD, and later arrivals such as Industrial Adhesives, Alcan-Ekco, Langlow Products and Excel Logistics. At the same time older industries and firms developed, like Webb Jarrett, Beechwoods, Spa Brushes, and George Tutill, Barnes and Giffard Newton.

'Meanwhile . . . significant [to] the future of Chesham, the Rotary Club had been formed in 1947 and Chesham Chamber of Trade & Commerce' a year later. In 1955 the Chamber mounted 'an ambitious Trades Fair' linking 'the former Darsham Hall . . . with a floored marquee' in Darvell's carpark off High Street. Security was tight and 'Two unwanted visitors on the second night were duly deposited in Skottowe's Pond'. Sixteen of those local managers at the Trades Fair formed Chesham Round Table 522. First officers were Peter Larkin as Chairman, Dick Askew of Carlton Press, Vice Chairman; John Ellis, estate agent, Secretary, Gerald Day of Van Houten as Treasurer and shoemaker Richard Barnes and Leslie Harborne of Brandon's stores first members of the ruling council. (There were additions within the founding year, including your editor.) The Table's fundraising activity started in 1956 with the Thatched Cottage which raised £147 for local charity. Thirty years later Table reported £37,766 raised by its Christmas floats. That original float graced the grounds of a children's hospital in Aylesbury as a Wendy House.

From manufacturing, Peter Larkin's memories turn to the local motor trade, so much a feature of post-war growth. Of the 'old established firm of C. Catling . . . Jim Catling . . . anticipated St Mary's Way by facing all new buildings towards Skottowe's Pond.' Jim Catling was also a Tabler and powered 'Santa's Christmas helicopter with an old Ford engine'. Then there were G. Marshall & Sons of Waterside, Nashleigh Garage, and E. Mulkern of Nashleigh Hill. 'At the foot of White Hill William Priest ran a motor repair shop and a public house. They moved to Latimer Road Garage where Albert Priest developed today's Priest's of Chesham.' Wally Fitch launched Fitch's Garage and W. E. Fitch & Sons. And then there was Doug McMinn — 'you must include his story' — who 'built the McMinn Centre'.

He also gave the first massive funds to the Stoke Mandeville Spinal Injuries Centre — a gesture which was anonymous at the time and about which nothing is heard these days — quiet giving, typical of the man and of his adoptive town.

That Chesham has changed cannot be disputed. One man well placed to observe that change is Sidney Chapman's sixties successor, High School headmaster Ken Stokes.

'The vigour, variety and, significantly, the charm of Chesham were more readily seen and appreciated in September 1966 than today. A first-time visitor had to negotiate a busy, cluttered High Street, with two-way traffic. The shops were intriguing — House of Tree, Gutteridge's et al, and moreover, one could 'window shop' from one's car as traffic moved fitfully through the Town'.

'That first visit was to be interviewed for the vacant Headship; no promise was made of buildings fit for the '60s let alone ones for the '90s! No promises were made for "Educational Developments", save the broad invitation — "Do whatever you can!". Local manufacturers were represented on the governing body, as they had been since the initial effort to generate "Technical Education" in the area, arising out of the 1944 Education Act, and it included William (Will or Bill) Moulder, a splendid link with the Town's past.

'I thought that I might stay for a few years, and then move on, possibly back to a Comprehensive School. In those days, the national trend was towards "Re-organisation" and only developments consistent with Comprehensive Education were given the benefit of government-approved building funding. Indeed, the School's first phases of building development, envisaged a Comprehensive

School emerging from the "Technical High".

'Within eighteen months, the school's case for development funds was accepted and began, this momentum was unstoppable, though none of the building phases were offered "on a plate", each of the eleven needing active lobbying.

'In 1967 local Secondary facilities (Cestreham & Lowndes, Raans and Brudenell, Challoner's Schools) were all relatively up-to-date, if not brand new; but all were single sex schools. The ensuing years have seen local moves towards Mixed Secondary schooling. Chesham High offered a viable, philosophically logical alternative form of Selective Education for Chesham and the wider area.

'I cannot view Chesham without thoughts about contacts with some 5,000 pupils, their families and their teachers, the many local people who offered help and support. The undoubted honour of having been Headmaster of Chesham High is compounded by working in and for Chesham itself . . . the development of Chesham High was an example of Chesham's seized opportunities. Chesham should cherish the Institutions which started here!'

Inevitably, it is professional scribes who observe with interest, affection, and a certain wry objectivity. Tony White is no exception. As Editor of the town's still independent newspaper, the *Bucks Examiner*, he has served for more years than any predecessor except the legendary Spec. An ardent soccer fan, his experience of Chesham was limited to two 'brief forays . . . to report on football matches' until 1967. Then he became Editor. He came with some foreboding: 'Chesham was known in the Vale as something of a frontier town, with grim warnings to stay away from The Broadway, or be prepared to face trouble.

'It didn't ring true that day in 1967. A quick pint in The Lamb, in the notorious Broadway, steadied my nerves before meeting the directors. It was a sunny day . . . what was all the fuss about? I wondered. And still do.

'My wife and I moved to Chesham in October 1967 and it was not too long before we decided this was where we wanted to bring up our children'. Why? 'The welcome from the people, not only my new employers, but also the many with whom we came into contact during those early months and years.

'Of those employers, two stand out, one still a good friend, though he now lives in Norfolk: Dick Askew, managing director of the *Examiner* until he retired in the late 1980s. Dick was a fair man, a man much involved in the community, who worked for many charities, and for local hospitals. One could not help but be influenced by his sense of what was right and wrong in the way he treated his fellows, including employees. The other was Leslie Livermore, deputy managing director for many years, a man who had steered the *Examiner* on a straight course for decades, and who had worked with five editors, including myself.

'Leslie Livermore it was, who made me very much aware of the achievements of my predecessors, including the legendary Frank 'Spec' Hiddleston, editor from 1904 until 1954, a record likely never to be matched. Following him there were Sandy Erskine, Clive Birch, and the man from whom I assumed the post, Derek Fowler.

'Early memories abound, particularly being taken by Derek to meet the clerk of the urban district council, Ivo Nash. I remember him sitting behind his desk, very correct, very knowledgeable, very old-worldly.

'Being a sports enthusiast, Chesham United took much of my attention throughout that first season. And why not? They were on a cup run, the dream of all clubs, and finally made it to the final of the FA Amateur Cup and Wembley. There can be nobody who was there who will ever forget being part of that 52,000 crowd on a beautiful April day, to see their local team walk up that famous tunnel and on to the unbelievably green and hallowed turf. All right, so they lost 1-0, but somehow it didn't seem to matter. This small-town football team had made history, even to the extent of being the subject for a famous sports cartoonist on the back page of one of the national newspapers.

'The town, which earlier that day was deserted as all the shops closed and most of the inhabitants made their way to Wembley by coach, train and car, was ready for the return in the evening. A balcony had been erected outside Brandon's. Thousands crammed the square, and welcomed the team back, empty-handed, but proud. Just wait until next season, they said. We did, but most of them left, and United were left with the task of finding a new team, even a new manager, for John Reardon, the man who had taken them to Wembley had, inexplicably, been sacked.

'Chesham Urban District Council was one of the best local authorities I had come across. Its record was good, in administering its own water works, its own council housing, sheltered housing . . . the list could go on. So one of the big, and I think sad, stories was that of its demise on the reform of local government in 1974, to be replaced by Chiltern District Council and, instead of a parish council as had been threatened, a town council. We then had a Town Mayor! It set in train the building of Elgiva Hall, funded from the sale of its water undertaking.

'Other outstanding memories include the way townspeople banded together to fight for what they believed should be theirs, including the threatened closure of the railway station, threats to their local general hospital at Amersham, a 24-hour police station (lost) and their main post office (lost). They fought to keep their fire station (won) . . . and will no doubt go on fighting.

'Perhaps one can best sum up local people by recalling a particular period when pensioners were continually falling victim to thieves. No sooner had the *Examiner* been on sale with a story of a pensioner having her savings stolen, then contributions, from ordinary people, young and old, would come into the front office. "Please pass this on" was the message, and it more than adequately illustrates why this is a good place to live and work.'

If Tony White is happy he found Chesham and stayed here, there are many who share his pleasure, but have had to leave. One such is the Suffragan Bishop of Hertford, the Rt Rev Robin Smith: 'Chesham was our home from 1972 - 1990, the place where our children grew up and which gave us so many memories we still treasure. Not all that remarkable to a casual observer, Chesham has a magnetic appeal: it is no accident that many who arrive as birds of passage feel impelled to stay. For it is a place with deep roots. With the old village at its heart and many residents whose links go back for generations, the town has a strong centre; and the independency of previous generations gives it a distinctive character to this day. Chesham will always command a very special place in our hearts.'

When all's said and done, it is the people of the place who shine through this necessarily selective but telling record, which in some measure saves our yesterdays for tomorrow's town. Tony Harman lives in Grove Farm, a moated manor house, which he restored. He has been a parliamentary candidate, councillor, magistrate, farmer, builder, author and broadcaster. He married a Plested and his children, grandchildren and great-grandchildren live, work and learn in Chesham. Few are better qualified to close this story of *A Chesham Century*.

'Because I am old, I cry for the little town, nestled in its narrow valley, and that has not struggled up the hills to the north and west. When Lords Mill, Cannon Mill and Weirhouse Mill still ground our corn along the river Chess, brought in from local farms. When the pens from the old cattle market were still there in Red Lion Street, not in my time in use, but there as a reminder that this had been a market town. When Church Street housed butcher and baker and families who had been there for generations, not a yuppie in sight. When the High Street was full of small shops and tradesmen who knew their trade and provided every possible service and article, each on an individual basis, when there was real competition. When the men came out from the newer roads in Newtown, in answer to the factory sirens to make boots and wonderful wooden ware, to fill the wagons in the station yard to go all over the country. When we had our own brewery, and our own gas works, each with the appropriate smell, and a local electric light company which boasted the man who must have been the tallest engineer in the whole industry, Mr Clayton. When there were innumerable pubs (how did they make a living?) and many many non-conformist chapels.

'Was it my imagination, or was the High Street on Saturdays and Sundays in the early '30s just filled with the most attractive girls that have ever been in history? In later life, a senior policeman told me that at that time, all the unmarried policemen in Bucks wanted to serve in Chesham, for the obvious reason. Oh yes, sex was around even in those days. Then our own Co-op was still growing and absorbing those of neighbouring towns, supported in the main by the same sturdy individuals who worked the local factories. The Hospital Fête was to me the height of annual entertainment. I expect it was a bit corny really.

'Then the whole world itself was so quiet, and the enthusiasm of local football crowds so intense, that I could sit three miles away, and hear the roar of the supporters of Chesham United, to the extent that some people could tell by its intensity, when the local star, Dicky Lacey, had the ball at his feet. The Club is still there, in a higher league than it used to be, but you can't hear the supporters from miles away because of the noise of the helicopters overhead, sometimes looking for prisoners who have escaped from Bovingdon, other times just enjoying themselves in their own noisy way, but just because I am old, I shouldn't mourn the passing of all these things, for so many things are better.

'The houses on the hill partly replace the slums of Star Yard, Townfield Yard, insanitary and cramped and unhealthy, which have long since gone. No longer do many, many young Chesham people have to spend part of their youth recovering from TB in special centres — and so many did not recover. No time for crying really. It is just that I am old'.

Yes, we are all older, and we all cry over bad times and for our good days long gone. Yet, as Chesham, Town and Council, looks back over this century of change and achievement, it also looks forward — to more change, some perhaps in local powers and those who serve, some certainly in the remorseless shifts of townscape.

Yet there remain two constants — Chesham still stands secure 'twixt field and meadow, bound fast by its iron-stream, guarded by the well ordered woodlands on its several skylines. And it rests, well-ordered and compleat within its unchanging spirit of independence, and its friendships, in chapel and in pub, at school or workbench, in terrace or villa, farm or flat, Native or newcomer, we all serve one another.

LEFT: Pubs like the Tap in the High Street, and Chesham's own brewery up White Hill, survived into the fifties. The horse was Grey Duke. (EB) RIGHT: The Queen's Head was renowned for its democracy and kind acts. BELOW: The Reynolds sisters ran the Primrose Cafe, and the sale of J. D. Dell was a sign of the changing times.

ABOVE: E. Climpson & Sons was the town's free vintner, heir to an old tavern tradition, and where many a pensioner enjoyed long credit.
BELOW: Germain Street in 1939 — when Ben Boughton went to school.

The Astoria fleapit, once Chesham Palace, shared billing with the Embassy. It became a furniture shop.

ABOVE: Pubs were where the deals were struck — like the New Inn down Waterside, in 1938. (SHF) BELOW: The Culverhouse family with Alice Rose's goat cart. (AH)

LEFT: Great events — the Webb Jarrett fire was one; this was the fire at Beechwood's in Higham Road between the wars. RIGHT: There were woods to play in — and paths like the lane from Chartridge to Asheridge in 1936. BELOW: Chalk Hill was 'just a cart track cut out of the hillside' — like this path above the town, on the Balks.

ABOVE: 'Later on they built a proper edge to the pond and put boats on it . . .' BELOW: 'Whip whip behind' was the cry when local lads hitched rides on the back of timber carts — here at Top Common, Hyde End. (SHF)

ABOVE: Thos Wright turned to tractor units like this soon after.
BELOW: The Waterside chip shop caught fire but the Fire Brigade soon took control.

ABOVE: The Larkin cartshed — the first workshop and its replacement, 1950s. (PL) BELOW: The Trades Fair which gave birth to Round Table: the brothers Derek, Alan and Peter, and their parents Fred and May, 1955. (HS/PC)

The Council celebrates — this was the opening of Hivings Park Free Church in 1962: Dennis Birch is in the doorway, Rev Eric Wood on the left, and co-author Arnold Baines extreme left, with Mrs Wood and Rev A. E. Wood, Mrs Nancy Clarke; Cllrs Will Moulder and Cyril Howard stand in the doorway.

LIST OF PAST CHAIRMEN AND MAYORS

E. REYNOLDS	1895-97	W. L. SILLS	1955-56
T. de FRAINE	1897-98	W. T. MOULDER	1956-57
D. G. PATTERSON	1898-99	MRS F. K. BRANDON	1957-58
E. REYNOLDS	1899-01	(née Rose)	
G. BARNES	1901-02	F. E. PEARCE	1958-59
J. HAYES	1902-03	W. T. MOULDER	1959-60
W. J. ABBOTT	1903-05	A. H. J. BAINES	1960-61
J. HERBERT	1905-06	F. O. BELL	1961-62
H. G. ROSE	1906-07	MRS F. A. CLARKE	1962-63
H. G. WEBB	1907-08	(née Clay)	
J. REYNOLDS	1908-09	F. M. HARRIES	1963-64
G. WALLINGTON	1909-10	W. T. MOULDER	1964-65
W. J. ABBOTT	1910-11	J. J. T. ROBERTS	1965-66
DR H. R. B. HICKMAN	1911-12	T. SCOTT	1966-67
F. E. HOWARD	1912-13	MRS K. L. HARRIES	1967-68
R. HOWARD	1913-14	W. L. SILLS	1968-69
W. J. HAYES	1914-15	A. C. SMITH	1969-70
H. A. V. BYRNE	1915-20	A. H. J. BAINES	1970-71
H. G. WEBB	1920-22	MRS K. L. HARRIES	1971-74
F. E. HOWARD	1922-23		
R. HOWARD	1923-24	**MAYORS**	
W. G. PAYNE	1924-25	W. L. SILLS	1974-75
H. G. ROSE	1925-26	A. P. BENNETT	1975-76
E. EAST	1926-27	C. J. F. DOWNS	1976-77
R. J. J. SWAN	1927-28	A. C. SMITH	1977-78
A. P. PATTERSON	1928-29	P. A. WARD	1978-79
F. E. HOWARD	1929-30	A. H. J. BAINES	1979-80
R. HOWARD	1930-31	MRS P. R. WILKINSON	1980-81
W. G. PAYNE	1931-32	N. L. BROWN	1981-82
A. P. PATTERSON	1932-33	MRS D. MULKERN	1982-83
R. HOWARD	1933-34	B. J. MELDRUM	1983-84
F. E. HOWARD	1934-36	MRS L. MOUNTAIN	1984-85
E. CULVERHOUSE	1936-37	F. J. MASON	1985-86
A. P. PATTERSON	1937-38	MRS J. E. FRANKS	1986-87
G. O. BELL	1938-47	MRS M. I. P. WALKER	1987-88
A. C. SAYWARD	1947-48	G. L. DIXON	1988-89
C. H. WILLIAMS	1948-49	C. P. GIBSON	1989-90
J. E. S. CLAPP	1949-50	MRS A. F. HOOKER	1990-91
F. G. PLUMMER	1950-51	MRS D. K. CARTER	1991-92
C. E. HOWARD	1951-52	(née Dayer)	
T. SCOTT	1952-53	A. T. KETTERINGHAM	1992-93
A. P. PATTERSON	1953-54	N. L. BROWN	1993-94
J. J. T. ROBERTS	1954-55	S. W. JAMES	1994-95

CLERKS OF THE COUNCIL

CHESHAM URBAN DISTRICT COUNCIL		CHESHAM TOWN COUNCIL	
Frederick How	1895-1899	Kenneth A. Marks	1974-1980
John Gibbon How	1899-1910	Ian W. Brown	1980-1989
William John Standring	1910-1924	Michael W. Kennedy	1989-
George S. Scott	1924-1931		
Bernard Blaser*	1931-1945	*(retired 31.12.1945)	
Walter Ivo Nash**	1946-1969	**(commenced 1.1.1946)	
George H. Malin	1969-1974		

INDEX

All figures in *italics* refer to illustrations

Abercrombie, Prof 71,121
Abingdon Abbey 13
Acts etc
  Commons, 1900 35,45
  Local Government 31,95
  Public Health, 1875 18,59
  Shops 47
  Sunday Fairs, 1448 14
  Third Reform 19
  Toleration 17
  Water, 1945 84
Admiralty 71
Ainley Taylor 107,109
Alan Jenkins & Associates 90
Alban, St 12
Alcan-Ekco 123
Alsi (Ælfsige, Æthelsige) 13
allotments 43,71,119
Americans 71,75
Amersham 13,14,18,77,83,109, 110,116,117,118
  Hospital 18,127
  Parish Council 95,96
  Poor Law Union 18,31
  Rural District Council .. 38,58,96
  Sanitary Authority 18,31
Archena 91,102
Armistice 51
Amy (Amen) Mill House *68*, 69,*94*,*97*,107
Asheridge 14
  Bottom 54,113,115
  Vale 54
Ashfield(s) 15,16
Ashley Green 14
  Parish of St John 35
Askew(s) 109
  Dick 123,125
Assessors of Taxes 36
Assoc of Municipal Corporations 95
Astoria cinema *131*
Atlas (pencils) 108
Aureole House 16,*23*
Aylesbury 116,117,124
Aylward, Rev A.J. 18
Baines, Arnold 109,*137*
Balks, the 17,*133*
Balliol, Master of 15
Baptist(s) 17,108
Barnes 16,107,123
  George 32
  Richard 123
Batchelor 16
Barnard, Mrs *67*
Bateman, E. *30*
Bates 16
Bayeux, Bishop of 14
Bayman Manor 69
BBC News 123
Beaconsfield 117
Bedford, Duke of 17,38,110
  Earl of 16
Beechwoods 123,*133*
'beer, boots & brushes' 107,112
Belgic 11
Bell, Geoffrey O. 8,59,70,72
Bellingdon 14,15,17,90
Berkhamsted 13,17,36,70,117
Bevan, Aneurin (Nye) 77,108
Bidwell 12
Big Round Green 82
Billeting Officer 70
Birch 16,110,127
  Clive 99,126
  Dennis *137*
Birinus, St 12
Biro, Val 83,108
Blaser, Bernard 70
Blease Medical Equipment 123
Blucher 17
Blundel, H.R. 70
Board of Agriculture & Fisheries 45

Boer War 113
Bois, de, family 15
Bolebec, Hugh de 14
Bone, F. *30*
'booke of Taxaton', 1606 2
Booth, Gen 47
Botley 14,15,60,83
  House 110
Boughton, Ben .... 110 *et seq*,*130*
  T.T. 111
  Uncle Tom 111
Bovingdon airfield 75
  prison 128
Brandon 16
  Mrs F.K. *8*,109
  (store) *33*,108,123,126
Brihtric 13
Britons 12,13
Broad, John 117
Broadwater Bridge 72
Broadway Farm 111
Broc Family 15
Brockhurst estate 44,51
Bronze Age 11
Brown's 119
Buchanan, Prof Sir Colin 80
Bucks CC .... 35 *et seq*
  Examiner 19,37,117,125,126
  Point lace 16,114
War Agricultural Committee 71
Burnham 13
Burns, Rt Hon John 43
Bury, the 17,*24*,*30*,33,75, 108,114
  Div HQ 118
  Farm 117,118
  Manor 15
Butt, Henry 32
Byrne, Henry 51
Caerda 15
Caesar, Julius 11
Cannon Mill 15,51,89,127
Canterbury, Archbishop of 13
Captain's Wood 13,82,113
  Scheme 36
Carlton Press 123
Carsberg 123
Catling(s) 109
  Billy 113
  C. 124
  farmyard 110
  Henry 32
  Jim 124
  Mr 119
Catuvellaunian(s) 12
Catherall, Dr 116
Cave Wood 122
Ceasteles-hamm 12
CCTV 102
Cestreham (Tsestresham, Cestresham) 14
chalybeate springs 12,*19*
Chalfont Road 86,111
  St Giles 111
Chance, Alice Mary 114
Chapman('s) 113
  Sidney 124
Chartridge 14,15,35,36
  Green *39*
  Parish Council 89
Cheddington 117
Chenies Manor Farm 110
  Mill 110
Chesdale Stores ....,....... 110
Chesham (Chessam) ..... 14 *passim*
  & Amersham Div Educational
    Exec 72
  Arts Soc 85
  Bois 60
  Boy Scouts 119
  Brass Band 38
  Brewery 83,*88*,118
  British Legion 51
    Restaurant 70
  Building Soc 17,107,113,114
  Burial Board 33
  Bury 15
  Carnival 109,119
  Cemetery 18,59,89,104
  Chamber of Trade 75,81,123
  Church Lads Brigade 119
  Clock Tower 90,91,*92*,100

  Co-op 48,69,72,128
  County Court 18
  Cricket Club 18
  engine shed 27
  Festival Committee 83
  Fire Brigade 17,*25*,46,49, 69,70,74,119,*135*
    engine *42*
    Station 46
  Gas Co 17
  Generals (General Baptist)
    FC 18,*30*,65
  Girl Guides 69,119
  goods yard *29*
  Higham 14,15
  Hospital Fête 114,119,128
  1000 Exhibition 83
  Infant Welfare Centre 51
  Isolation Hospital 38
  Liberal Assoc 80
  Library 70
  Lord .. 18,33,35,38,45,59,60,110
  Palace *131*
  Parish Council 89,96
  Property Owners' Assoc 114
  Ratepayers' Assoc . 46,59,80,114
  Rectory 17
  Rotary 80,109,123
  Round Table 80,109,123
  School Board 17,31,33
  Sea Cadets 83
  Skating Rink 70
  Silver Prize Band 57,72
  Society 81,83
  Tapestry 85
  Town Band 77
    Council .... 89 *et seq*,96
  Football Club 18,*107*
  Townswomen's Guild 80,81
  Trades Fair 123
  UDC .... 18 *passim*
  United FC 126,128
  Vale 15,67,117
    industry *93*
  Vicarage *20*
  Woburn 17
  Youth Clubs 119
    Council 91,101
Chessmount Estate 77
Chess River 11,12,*21*,45, 50,58,72,89,114,127
  Sports & Leisure Assoc 90
  Valley 11,60
  Arch & Hist Soc 83
Chestleham 14
Cheyne family 15
Chilton, Henry 32
Chiltern(s) 11,72,121
  Conference 82
  District Council 84,89,90,100
  Forest 13
  Hills 11
  Hundreds 60
  Housing Assoc 44,76
chip shop fire *135*
Chittenden, Leo 108
Cholesbury 11,60
Common *106*
Chorleywood 111
churches, chapels etc.
  Broadway General Baptist ... 17, 22
  Chesham Bois 114
  Christ Church 18,*29*
  Congregational 17,56
  Hinton Baptist 58
  Hivings Park Free 56,79,*137*
  Lower Baptist meeting 12
  Parish 12
  Presbyterian 17
  St Mary's 12,14,15,17,18, *20*,*30*,83,85
  Tylers Hill 33
  Townfield Baptist 56
  Trinity 17,56
  United Reformed 17
  Zion Baptist schoolroom *74*
Churchill, Winston 108
Citizens' Advice Bureau 75
Civic Trust award 89
Civil War 17
Clapp JP, J.E.S. 108
Clarke, Albert 54

field boots 116	(Ælfgifu), Lady 13,*21*,83	Harries, Kath *8*,85,120
Mrs 111	Elizabeth II 76	Harvest festival *74*
Nancy *137*	Ellis, John 108,123	Haslehurst, Nancy 117
Clay's, butcher 111	Embassy Cinema *68*,107,112	Hawes, W. *30*
Clayton, Mr 128	Emmanuel kilns 16	Hawkes 16,44
Clement Davies Committee 71	Equity Hall *67*,70,75	Ernie 111
Climpson('s) *88*	Erskine, Sandy 126	Hawkins, Gaius 32
E. & Sons *130*	Ethelwold, St 13	Hawridge 11
Jim 109	Evacuation Committee 70	health centre 84
coat of arms 82	Excel Logistics 123	Hearn 16
Cocke 16	FA Amateur Cup 126	H. & Son 122,123
Codmore Field 82,91	Fairs 38,58,121	Harry 111,112
Commons Preservation Soc 35	Cattle 14	Kitty 107,108
Community Relations	Cherry 14	Hemel Hempstead 17,113,118
Council 79	Statty (hiring) 14	Heistercamp, Camille 117
Comps 13	Faithorn, Dr 18	Herbert, Charles 32
Constables 36,60	Festival of Britain 76	Herbert's Hole 12
constituency 83	Chesham 83	Hertford, Suffragan Bishop
Co-op Field 82	Fewtrell, Det Supt Malcom...115,116	of 12*7*
Hall 70,109	Financial Clerk 46	Hiddleston, Frank 'Spec' *67*,
Cope, Johnny 111	Fitch, Wally 124	108,117,118,126
Coronation Day 76	W.E. & Sons 124	Higham Mead 123
Coulson, Sgt Bob 108	Flight Equipment 123	High Court 59,121
Council Chamber 75,83	Flying Service	Level water supply 36,37,*40*
Offices 99,101	Engineering 123	Sheriff 17,67,76
Room 36,46	Food Control Committee 51	Wycombe 113
Tax 104	Office 75	Hilltop Co 56
County Hall 109	Forelands 16,71	estate 110,122
Covent Garden 116	Forestry Commission 74	Hinchcliffe, Capt. 51
Cow Meadows 72	Fowler, Derek 126	Hivac 123
Cox, Stan(ley) 108,116,118	Fraine, Thomas Turner de 32	Hodgkins, Ron 115
Wilf(red) 107,111,112,	Francis, John 110	Honeysuckle Field 59
113,116	Freeman, George 32,33	Hooker, Mrs A.F. 91
crafts 16,18,*26*,107	Friedrichsdorf 91,102	Horsnell, Alison .... 113 *et seq*
crematorium 77	Frith, Francis *30*	House of Commons 4*3*
Cromwell House 85	Fuller(s) 17	of Tree 108,124
Crossrail project 103,*105*	*Future For Chesham, A* 81	Housing development
Culpin, Clifford 79,84	Gallipoli gun 51,*53*	1954-73 77,78,79
Culverhouse,	Gardner 16	Manager *72*
Alison Rose 113,*132*	Garlick's *97*	Schemes 121
Edward 113,114	Garrett-Pegge, Mr 35,57	How 16
Edward John 113,114	Miss C.J. 89	Ernie 116
family *132*	J.R 89	Frederick 31
Henry Robert 113,114	JP 108,116	Howard 16
Cumbers 12	Gate 16	Cyril 109,116,*137*
Danes 14	Geary 44	F.E. *8*,52,67,72,75
Dark Ages 12	George V, King 47,58	Phil 117
Darsham Hall 123	VI 76	Ralph 58,60,69
Darvell ('s) 16,108,123	Germains 12,17,108	Hundridge 14,15
Joe 111	Germanic 12	Hyde House 17
Davis, W.J. 70	Germans 72,108	Industrial Adhesives 123
Dawes, Miss 77	Gerrards Cross 116,117	inns, hotels etc.
Day, Gerald 123	Gibbons, Henry James 32	Blue Ball 108
Days & Moments 118	Gilbert('s) Taxis *53*	Crown 108
Dean, Dixie 107	& Sullivan 107	George Hotel 32
Helen 107	Gladstone, Mr 19,31	Golden Ball 16,*23*,111
Deansway House 79,80	Glenthorne 114	Lamb 125
Deland, P.L. 60	Glorious Revolution 17	Last Post 16
Dell 16	Godwin, Earl 13	Nag's Head 57,*63*
J.D. *129*	Gomm 16	Nash (leigh Arms) 110
Miss 59	Robert .... 118 *et seq*	Plough *88*
Denner Hill(ing) 38	S. *30*	Queen's Head (Lizzie's
Dept of the Environment 95	Gooding's smithy *68*,70,109	Bonce) 108,*129*
Derrick's 107	Gray, Sir Edward 47	New Inn *132*
Dodd, John 110	Great Hivings estate 56,122	Red Lion 57,62,*63*
Mr 118	Missenden 118	Sun Lodging-house 16,22
Sarah 110	Rebuilding 16,*22*	Tap 108,*129*
Domesday Survey 14,60	Train Robbers 117	Three Tuns 82,*88*,123
Dominions 71	Green Belt 82,113	Iron Age 11,12
Door Porter 36	Greenham, Eddie 117	Early 11
Dormer, Percy 44	Grey Duke *129*	Isene, river 12,*19*
D'Oyly Carte 109	Griffiths, Griff 107	Ivinghoe Beacon 11
Drill Hall 83	Grosstephan, (Miss) 108	Jackson, Cdr Fred 109,116
Dungrove 11,37,76,82,114	Grove, Mr & Mrs Ben 115	James, Steve *7*
field 15	Farm 127	John Kay House 85
view from *8*,*53*	Manor 15	Joint Burial Committee 36,45,
Dwight 16	Grover 16	59,89,96
F. *30*	A.F. 123	Kay, Frederick 123
Earl Marshall 82	Miss 112	Keen's dairy 115
East('s) *26*	Guide Commissioner *67*	Kennedy, Mike 99
Ebenezer Cottages 12	Hut *67*	Kent 11
Edith, Queen 13	Gumdrop 108	Kesters 14
Edgar, King 13	Gutteridge 109,124	King 44
Edgware 123	Hadrian, Emperor 12	Kingham's 116
Edward the Confessor 13	Halton, RAF band 119	King's Royal Rifles 47,*52*
VIII *67*	hamlets 14	Kitty's Bridge 58
Edwy, King 13	Harborne, Leslie 123	Kress, Laurie 108
EEC 111	Harding 16	Labour 107
Elbourn, Ted *26*	Thomas 15	Exchange 75
election, 1894 31	Handpost Meadow 35	Lacey, Dicky 128
Electricity corner 109	Harman (Builders) Ltd 90	Ladysmith 113
Elgiva (Theatre) Hall 37,84,	Tony .... 127 *et seq*	Langlow Products 123
89,91,*92*,100,103,126	Harold, Earl; King 1*3*	Larkin(s) 109

140

Alan 136	Farm 70	Ranfurly, Hermione, Countess...121
cartshed 136	Millenary 83	Ratepayer 107
Derek 136	Mineral Cottage 19	Reading 16
Distribution Services 123	Ministry of Health 54,55	Reardon, John 126
Forge Ltd 122	Housing & Local	'Rec', the 35,110
Fred 122,136	Government 81,122	Reformation 15
May 136	Town & Country Planning ... 72	Reg of Derrick's 107
Peter .... 122 et seq,136	Transport 69,81	Reynolds 16,44
Latimer 10,12,14,15,16,35,	Missenden Abbey 15	Edwin 32,33
36,39,60,111,118	Mitchell, W.B. 72	sisters 129
Bottom 57	Moor, The 13,19,29,33,34,35,	Tessa 108
Road Garage 124	45,58,60,72,82,89,100,110	W. 30
Lee Common 11	Lower 89	Richardson, W. 30
The 15	Morris, Bryn(dley) 108	Rickmansworth 118
Leicester Abbey 17	Morrison, Miss Jane 114	& Uxbridge Valley Water
Leisure Centre 90,100	Moss, Anthony 118	Co 36,84
Lewin (Leofwine), Earl 13	Frank 54,69,70	Risborough 13
Ley Hill 15,33,60,83	Moulder, A. 30	Road Foreman 46
1920s 10	Jesse 26	Robinson, George 67
Liberal 107	William 8,54,67,109,115,	Rolling Pin 75
Library, County 75,79	124,137	Roman 10,11,12,117
Limes site 79,80,81	Mozart Players 83	Romano-British 12
Livermore, Leslie 126	Mulkern, E. 124	Rose, Dicky (Dickinson) 107
Local Board of Health....18,31,32,75	Nap, the 12,20	Henry Glenister 32,58
Government Board 35,43,44	Nash, Billy 108	Mr 37
Review 100,102	W. Ivo 72,121,122,126	Rothschild(s) 53
Lollards 15,17	Nashleigh Garage 124	Lionel de, MP 43
Longstone Investments 90	Recreation Ground 58,59,71,	Walter, MP 37
Loosley 13	121	Rover 'bus 110
London 13,16,103,112,119	Neal, Supt John 116	Royal & Ancient Order of
& Birmingham Railway 80	Neolithic 11	Buffaloes 63
Sheriff 118	Newman, F. 30	Bucks Hussars 53
Transport 109	New Stone Age 11	Laundry 109
Long family 53	Newton, Giffard 107,123	'Rule 20' 36
Dr Freeman 44,59	Newtown 18,51,72,128	Russell, George 32,33
Lord's Mill 13,14,21,37,45,	Nonconformists 17	Sabatini 44
94,107,110,127	Norman Conquest 13	St Albans 12
L'Oreal 123	Northolt 112	John Medical Comforts 118
Loudwater 111	Nuisances, Inspector of ... 38,45,46	Mary de Pre 17
Loveday, Mr 111	old malt house 72,83	Mary's Church Rooms 31
Lower Bois 60	Orgill, O. 30	Salvation Army 47,58
Lowndes family 17,24,75,76,	Old Bailey 118	Sanitary Inspector 38
108	People's Welfare	Sarratt 111
JP 116	Committee 79	Saturley, L.D. 72,79
Squire 118	Olympic bobsleigh 108	Savings Bank 18
William 32,33,37,49	Ottaway, George 119	Saxon 12,13,19,28
W.F. 57,58,67,69,80	Overseers 33,36,60	Sayward, A.C. 71
Lye Green 15,60,82,83	Oxford, Earl(s) of 14,15	schools etc.
McIlroy, Sgt 108	Parish Council 33	Board 17
McMinn Centre 124	Park, the/Lowndes 14,17,20,	British 17,55
Douglas 90,108,116,124	37,49,57,76,80,89,110,118,119	Brudenell 125
Mafeking 113	Lower 65,66,75,76	Cestreham 11,83,125
relief of 82	Avenue 17,37,51,75,76,85	Challoners 112,125
Maison Melville 117	rose arbour 72,73	Chesham Park Community
Malin, George 85	Second 114,118	College 75
Malt House 84,88,89,101,104	Upper 75	College of FE 11
Treaty 89	Patterson, Andrew 8,69,109	Germain Street 112,118
Mapletree Farm 57	D.G. 37	Girls 18
Marble Arch 111	patronal feast (Assumption) 14	Governors, Grammar 47
Marina, Princess 79	Paxton, Fred 69	Heritage House 79
Market 14	Payne's Farm 69	High 83,100,125
House/Hall 18,21,82,90	Pearce 16,44,113	Infants 18
clock 46	Murky 109	Lowndes 75,108,125
Marks, Ken 84	Pednor 15,16,22	Raans 124
& Spencer 101	Penn 116	(St Mary's) National 17,21,60
Marshall, Gilbert 32	Pest Houses 115	& Sunday 50
G. & Sons 124	'Picturesque Bucks' 34	Technical 72
Marston Field 82,100	Piggin, George 113	Thomas Harding 17
Matthews, H.G. 90	Plested 108,128	Townsend Road Girls .. 25,43,93
Mayo, ... 44	Plummer, F.G. 58	White Hill ... 33,57,114,116,118
F. 30	Police Court 116	Scollay, Alan 109
& Hawkes 110	Station 18,24,102,106,	Scott, G.S. 55
Mayor .... 7,31,43,99 et seq	116,127	Tom 85
Mechanics' Inst 17,32,36	Pond Park 36,54,55,115	Seabrook, Michael 18
Medley 44	Pooley, Fred 80	Sewage Farm 37,54,83
Mead 16	Post Office 16,111,127	Sexton(s) 17
Edwin 32	Powell, L.C. 71	Shackman 123
Jesse 43	Priest(s), Albert 124	Reuben 108
Melville, Col Andy 108	of Chesham 124	Shardeloes 114
family 117	William 124	Sherman 111
Turkeys 118	Primrose Café 108,129	Shillakers 117
Mercia, King of 13	prisoners of war 72,121	Ship Money 17
Mesolithic 11	Puddephatt 108	Showmen's Guild 121
Metropolitan & Great	pudding stones 12	Sibley, William 32
Central 59	Puffa, Seric 15	Sixpenny Houses 76
Drinking Fountain & Cattle	Pug, Geoffrey 15	skating 66
Trough Assoc 43	Queen of Angels 75	Skottowe('s), Coulson 17
M1 motorway 110	Racklyeft ('s), Frederick 32	Philip 76
M15 108,118	Estate 56	Pond 45,57,59,65,66,76,
Middle Ages 15	railway line 86	81,114,118,123,134
Stone Age 11	station 127	slipes/slypes 17
Middlesex 12	Raison, Timothy, MP 95	Slough 113
Milk Hall 18,57	Rance 44	Smith, George James 32

Dr 67	King Street 44	Town Needs a Town Council, A 95
of Derby 90	Lansdowne Road 54	Townfield warden 77
Robin, Rt Rev 127	London Road 63	Tree Council 89
Spa 12	Lowndes Avenue 56,64	Scheme 89
Brushes 123	Lum's Yard 28	Warden 89
SPD 123	Lye Green Road 70	Traffic Commissioner 56
steam power 27	Lyndhurst Road 54	Treasury, HM 122
shuttle 86,105	Manor Road 54	Tree, Kath 108
Stephenson, A.T. 30	Way 56,70	Treiber, Nettie 109
Steward of Manors 38	Market Square 14,21,54,56	Solly 109
Stillman, Tilly 107	57,61,82,87	Tring 17,117
Stoke Mandeville Spinal	Meades Water Gardens 89	'bus 56
Injuries Centre 124	Milton Road 55	Trivial Round, the Common Task,
Stokes, Ken .... 124 et seq	Mineral Lane 122	The 108
Stone Age 10	Missenden Road ... 12,71,77,121	Tutill, George 123
(Old) 11	Moor Road ('China') 37	Tylers Hill 16
straw-plait 16	Mount Nugent 17	UBM-Pratt site 101,104
streets, roads etc.	Nashleigh Hill 35,76,124	Ulyett, Phyl 108
Albany Court 114	New Road 46,123	Ray 108
Alexander Street 79	Nightingale 54	Unitary Authority 101
Alma Road 18	Overdale Road 54	Upper Moor 45
Amersham Road 46,57	Park Road 46,110	Urban District Councils
Amy (Amen) Lane 18,123	Parsonage Lane 55	Assoc 95
Asheridge Road 122,123	Patterson Road 77	Van Houten 118,123
Backs, the 113	Pednor Road 117,118	Vere, de 14
Beechcroft Road 77	Pednormead End 16	Hugh de 14
Beech Tree Hill 37	Penn Avenue 56,77	Verulamium 14
Bellingdon Road 38,56,71,	Pound, the 44,48,57	Vestry 16,31,33
73,76,112,114,121	Ramscote Lane 17	Victoria, Queen 38
Belmont Road 56	Red Lion Corner 37,42	Ville de Houilles 91,102
Benham Close 72,115	Street 57,111,127	Waitrose 101,112
Berkhampstead Road 36,37,	Gardens 57,76	Wallace 119
45,64	Relief Road 122	Wallington 111
Berkeley Avenue 77	Ridgeway Road 56,77	lemonade 123
Blucher Street 81	Riverside Court 83	George 32,38
Bois Moor Road 110,111	Terrace 37,41	War Memorial 51,61,62,76,89
Bottom Lane 57	Walk 89	Office 51
Breda Avenue 56,64	Ryecroft Road 77	Ware, John 17
Broadway 34,43,48,51,57,	St Mary's Way 51,83,87,112,	Warrender, Alice 69
59,61,64,67,69,72,75,107,108,	122,124	Washcock Wood 77
109,111,112,119,120,125	Severalls Avenue 37,51,65	watercress 12,116
Broad Street 37,52,64,81,	Shantung Place 37	Waterloo 17
110,116	Slypes, the 114	water power 27
Brockhurst Road 63,65	Springfield Road 122	Water Inspector 45
Bury Lane 12,47,76	Star Yard ... 28,34,57,64,118,128	Waterside 14,32,36,51,55,60,
Cameron Road 43,77	Station Road 37,44,112	79,89,116
Chalk Hill 115,133	Stratford's Yard 11,55	Waterworks 18,40,89
Chartridge Lane 46,56,120	Townfield (Yard) 17,37,55,	Watford 17,113
- Asheridge lane 133	56,85,129	Watts, Edwin 32,44
Chequers Yard 54	Trapps Lane 114	Webb 16
Chesham Bottom 37	Tylers Hill Road 57	George 32,33
Chessbury Road 77	Unicorn Hill 56	Jarrett 114,123,133
Chessmount Rise 56,71,122	Upland Avenue 55	Weedon Almshouses 16
Chess Valley Walk 89	Vale Road 37	family 15,16
Chesterton Close 55	Waterside 13,14,18,21,34,	Richard 16
Church Street 12,14,16,17,	123,124,132,135	Thomas 16
20,22,57,81,108,110,128	Wey Lane 12	Weir House Mill 59,127
Codmore Cross 37,40,72	White Hill 14,15,31,81,82,87,	Wellington, Duke of 17
Cowper Road 55	88,112,120,123,124,129	Wembley 126
Cromwell Terrace 85	footpath 87	Wendy House 124
Darsham Walk 28	Lion Yard 55	Wessex, King of 13
Dawes Close 12,77	Windsor Road 77	Weylands (poorhouse) 18,70
Deansway 77,115	Woodley Hill 56	Whelpley Hill 15
Delmeade Road 77	Stuart, Ted (Tchaikowsky) 108	Whichcote(s) 17
Duck Alley 37,41,55,113	Sundt 123	Whig 17
East Street 11,87	Surveyor & Waterworks	White, Tony .... 125 et seq
Eskdale Avenue 43,46,48,123	Engineer 46	Wilkins 111
Road 37,40	Swimming Baths (pool) 45,100	W. 30
Essex Road 37	Talbot, Dave 107	Willesden, Borough of 71
Eunice Grove 123	Taylor's Farm 38,48	Self-build Housing Assoc 77
Franchise Street 19	Tedworth, HMS 71	William I 13
Fryer Close 56	Tesco 103	Williams, George 118
Fullers Close 85	Temperance Hall 18,79,89	Windsor Castle 16
Hill 72,73,77,109	Soc. 38	Wing, Harry 111,112
George Street 79	Thames Conservancy 45,54,59	Wise, Dr Tom 108
Germain Street 16,68,70,81,	Valley 11	Woburn Abbey 17
109,110,112,119,130	Thatched Cottage 124	Wood, Mrs 137
Gordon Road 37	Thorn, A. 30	Rev A.E. 137
Gladstone Road 19,37,115	timber cart 134	Woodley, James 32
Green Lane 67	Times, The 117	Woodstock 44
Hampden Avenue 56	Tomlin, George 111	Woolworth 15
Hearn's Yard 46	Top Common, Hyde End 134	Wright(s) 16,107
Higham Road 40,133	Town Bridge 50	F. 30
Highfield Road 52	Clock 122	Jesse 32
High Street 14,36,50,51,57,	Crier 38,117	Thos 26,135
64,69,72,81,86,90,91,98,	Field 13,16	Wulfric 15
100,101,109,110,111,113,117,	Guide 75	WVS 69,75
121,123,124,128,129	Hall 18,21,43,46,49,57,60,	Wycombe 33
Hivings Hill 111,115	71,80,81,82,86,92,107	Wycliffe, Dr John 15
Howard Road 77	Map 80,82	Wykeridge 15
Hyatt's Yard 14	Museum 103	Yorke, Charlie 108
Khartoum Avenue 37,40,43,	Pump 43,48	Young, John 83
46,48	trough 48	

142

SUBSCRIBERS

Presentation copies

1 Chesham Town Council
2 Chiltern District Council
3 Buckinghamshire County Council
4 Chesham Library
5 Buckinghamshire County Records Office

6 Dr Arnold H. J. Baines
7 Stephen W. James
8 Michael W. Kennedy
9 George H. Malin
10 Bernard J. Meldrum
11 John Armistead
12 Irene Brown
13 Clive & Carolyn Birch
14 Peter Jones
15 Jack Newell
16 Max Jones
17 The Chesham Society
18 W. J. Martin
19 Ron How
20 Waterside County Combined School
21 S.E. Bloss
22 T.J. & K.M. Andrew
23 Tony White
24 David & Jill McCluney
25 Mrs A. Franklin
26 P.W. Willoughby
27 M. Willoughby-Zahid
28 W.E. Stannard
29 Melanie Jane Bettridge
30 Jeanette Stearn
31 Laszlo L. Grof
32 R. Hodgkins
33 Mrs A. Quinnell
34 Mrs M. Bicknell
35 D. Patterson
36 P. Read
37 E. Smeed
38 J. Lovett
39 E. Bartlett
40 F.W. Kerr
41 R. Parrin
42 M. Parsons
43 Mrs B.V. Veale, Elmtree County First School
44 F.J. Bunker
45 Mrs E.R. Phillips
46 Mr & Mrs J.A. Clark
47 Mrs M. Edwards
48 Gordon L. Dixon
49 L.S. Disspain
50 Marjorie E. Bell
51 Keith E. Fletcher
52 Anthony Collins
53 Peter Cuthbert
54 H.R. & E.W. King
55 Dr & Mrs C.A. Foxell
56 J.L. Howard
57 W.J. Howard
58 Edward Darvell
59 Mrs C.G. Rickett
60 R.J. White
61 Norman H. Norris
62 G.R. Hawkes
63 Rev Alan & Mrs Janet Davis
64 Ann & Geoff Parr
65 Mrs Anita Richadson
66 Mr & Mrs W.T. Hailey
67 M.C. Cooper & S. Peskin
68 Ann Huckett
69 R.J. Jenner
70 Percy & Audrey Matthews
71 Myra Ann Tricker
72 Bryan Pearson
73 Gary M. How
74 N.F. Pearce
75 Rt Rev Leonard Ashton
76 Mr & Mrs M. Puzey
77 Tony & Wyn White
78 Mrs Steve Shirley
79 W.G. Mayo
80 Mr & Mrs G.M. Povey
81 Graham Keith Thorn
82 T.G. Jeacock
83 J.M. Jeacock
84 Norah Podbury
85 Charles D. Chaney
86 Trevor Edwards
87 Mrs M.B. Leggett
88 Jonathan Simon Miller
89 Catherine Miller
90 Redvers B.C. England
91 George Piggin
92 N.A. Mead
93 O.M. Biddiscombe
94 Clare Butler & Andy John
95 Mrs M.J. Larkin
96 Mrs V. Larkin
97 Mr & Mrs P.J. Larkin
98 Dr D.M.L Goodgame
99 Rev Andrew Warburton
100 Miss C. Robinson
101 Malcolm Fewtrell
102- Chesham Town
104   Museum Project
105 John & Derry Taylor
106 Stuart Matthews
107 A. Sedgwick
108 G. G.R. Wilson
109 All The Staff at Chesham Station
110 R. Richards
111 Edward Bunkham
112 Arthur T.F. Reynolds
113 David A.J. Reynolds
114 Paul T. Reynolds
115 Timothy F. Reynolds
116 Margaret Drinkwater
117 Mrs M.E. Hyland
118 A.E. Adams
119 Miss Culverhouse
120- Mrs W. Wright
121
122 Peter Vonwiller
123 Yasmin Ahmed
124 Cllr Derek Lacey, Dep Town Mayor & Mrs Trudy Lacey
125 Graham Edward Green
126 Paul & Janet Conway
127 Ivy May Green
128 His Honour Judge P.R. Simpson
129 Rex Lacey
130 P.C. Miller
131 Bert Darvell
132 Mr & Mrs W.D. Pratchett

133 Colin J. Seabright
134 Mr & Mrs M.R. Sawyer
135 Mr & Mrs G.H. Malin
136 Roderick Stewart Guthrie
137 Philip Lawson
138 Monica Murphy
139 John F. Parrott
140 P.F. Cansdale
141 Joyce Cooper
142 WgCdr Noel Archer OBE
143 John How
144 Mr & Mrs Anthony Moss
145 Andrew Stearn
146 Jeannette Lee
147 R.G. Darvell
148 M. Thomson
149 Ken Stokes
150-151 H.G. (Ben) Boughton
152-153 Mrs S.M. Evans
154 P.R. Honour
155 M.C. Belsham
156 Dr Arnold H.J. Baines
157 Cllr Mrs N.H. Downs
158 Brenda & Mike Kennedy
159 Chloe Kennedy
160 Laurence Kennedy
161 Freda & Oswald Kennedy
162 Alan Bacon
163 Noel Brown
164 Ian Campbell
165 Lesley Stearn
166 Mrs D. MacDonald
167 Andrew Ketteringham
168 Cllr Alan Walters
169 Dorothea Kathleen Carter
170 Cllr & Mrs C.P. Gibson
171 Mrs M. Walker
172 Margaret Weavers
173 Irene & Michael Brown
174 J.A. Hawkins
175 Bernard J. Meldrum
176 Ian Meldrum
177 Keith Meldrum

178 Mrs B. Meldrum
179 Shirley Gardiner
180 Thomas Harding County Middle School
181 Brushwood Middle School
182 Chesham High School
183 The William Durrant County Middle School
184 Albert Smith
185 Steve James
186 Wesley James
187 Jennifer & Rod Wallace
188 Betty & Trevor Beresford
189 Linda Gabriel
190 Nancy Seymour
191 Irene Seymour
192 Mr & Mrs I.P. Fewtrell-Smith
193 Mrs O.D. Palmer
194 Mr & Mrs J.F. Dedman
195 Mrs L.E. Smith
196 Mr & Mrs G.J. Hearn
197 Ken & Margaret Austin
198 Jo Franks
199-218 Chesham Town Council
219 Mr & Mrs W.T. Hailey
220 Jean B. Ladlay
221 Barry Collins
222 B.J. Waterman
223-224 Christopher Boulter
225 Ray East
226 Mrs A. Sheppard
227 Donal W. Flitney
228 Ronnie Rivans
229 Mrs B. Whitbread
230 Mrs A. English
231 The Park Club
232 R.F.G. Stratford
233 Brian Hunnibell
234 Marcus Hunnibell
235 Paul R. Smith
236 Mrs S.J. Kelsey
237 R.E. Mitchell
238 Mrs J. Knifton
239 Myra Webb
240 I. & E.A. Bateman

241 John Nash
242 David Haddock
243 Mrs M. Silver
244 Mrs M. Batchelor
245 Ian Miller
246 Colin Beattie
247 Miss S.M. Milton
248 Margaret Davies
249 Hilda Stevens
250 E.E. Hinks
251 Mrs E.C. Turney
252 Rod Culverhouse
253 Mrs A.R. Horsmell
254 Frederick Wilson
255 T.M. Shaddock
256 Mrs C.M. Ward
257 Mrs R. Wood
258 Rev Tony Meek
259 Douglas P. Deland
260 Mrs M. Heywood
261 Mrs M. Blake
262 R.W. Freeman
263 Mrs I. Bishop
264 R. & M. Edwards
265 Mr & Mrs R. Lee
266 Desmond John Simonds
267 Mr H.R. & Mrs M.J. Spillett
268 R.E. Hanna ISM ISO & Mrs E.W. Hanna
269 Penny Waterfall
270 William John Witney
271 Jean & Harold Atkins
272 Mr & Mrs C. Davis
273 Mr & Mrs Neil J. Packer
274 P.E. Cansdale
275 Peter Ward
276 Cllr Mrs Joan Baker
277 Mr & Mrs W.J. Leach
278 Elinor & Philippa Green
279 Cllr Bernard M. Curson
280 Cllr Peter W. Terrell
281 Mr & Mrs J.R.N. Croot
282 Mr & Mrs N.F. Grantham
283 Miss R.E.M. Purton
284-383 Chesham Town Council
384 Mrs S.D. Hodgkinson

Remaining names unlisted.